ARAB ARMOUR
VS
ISRAELI ARMOUR
Six-Day War 1967

CHRIS McNAB

OSPREY PUBLISHING
Bloomsbury Publishing Plc

Kemp House, Chawley Park, Cumnor Hill, Oxford OX2 9PH, UK
29 Earlsfort Terrace, Dublin 2, Ireland
1385 Broadway, 5th Floor, New York, NY 10018, USA
Email: info@ospreypublishing.com
www.ospreypublishing.com

OSPREY is a trademark of Osprey Publishing Ltd

First published in Great Britain in 2021
Transferred to digital print in 2024

A catalogue record for this book is available from the British Library.

Print ISBN: 978 1 4728 4287 9
ePub: 978 1 4728 4289 3
ePDF: 978 1 4728 4288 6
XML: 978 1 4728 4290 9

Artworks by Jim Laurier
Maps by www.bounford.com
Index by Angela Hall
Typeset by PDQ Digital Media Solutions, Bungay, UK
Printed and bound in India by Replika Press Private Ltd.

24 25 26 27 28   10 9 8 7 6 5 4 3

Artist's note

Readers can find out more about the work of illustrator Jim Laurier via the
following website: www.jimlaurier.com

Author's acknowledgements

I would like to thank Eliezer Avni of the Yad Lashiryon Association
Information Center, for clarifying some technical points, and editor
Nikolai Bogdanovic for his patient accommodations during the writing stages.

The Woodland Trust

Osprey Publishing supports the Woodland Trust, the UK's leading woodland
conservation charity.

www.ospreypublishing.com

To find out more about our authors and books visit our website. Here you
will find extracts, author interviews, details of forthcoming events and the
option to sign-up for our newsletter.

Editor's note

For ease of comparison of measurements, please refer to the following
conversion table:
1mm = 0.04in.
1cm = 0.39in.
1m = 3ft 3.3in.
1kg = 2lb 3.2oz
1 tonne = 1.1 US (short) ton
1 litre (L) = 0.22 gallon

Abbreviations

AA	anti-aircraft
ACV	armoured combat vehicle
APC	armoured personnel carrier
APHE	armour-piercing high-explosive
AT	anti-tank
CAS	close air support
GPS	gunner's primary sight
HE	high-explosive
HEAT	high-explosive anti-tank
HESH-T	high-explosive squash head tracer
HVAP	high-velocity armour-piercing
HVSS	horizontal volute spring suspension
IAF	Israeli Air Force
IDF	Israel Defense Forces
MBT	main battle tank
MG	machine gun
NBC	nuclear, biological, chemical
PLO	Palestine Liberation Organization
RHA	rolled homogenous armour
VVSS	vertical volute spring suspension

Front cover, above: An Egyptian T-54A on the Sinai Front, 1967. (Jim Laurier)
Front cover, below: An Israeli M50 Super Sherman of the 8th Armored
Brigade destroys a dug-in Syrian Panzer IV Ausf. H in the Tel Fahr position on
the Golan Heights, 1967. (Jim Laurier)
Title page image: A unit of IDF Centurion tanks moves through the Negev
Desert. (Fritz Cohen/Government Press Office (Israel)/CC BY-SA 3.0)

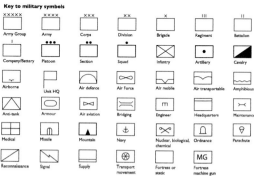

CONTENTS

INTRODUCTION

The Six-Day War of June 1967 stands as a true landmark in post-1945 military history. To this day, students and researchers in military colleges around the world study the conflict with intensity, scouring both strategy and tactics for the magical ingredients of that most elusive of military objectives – a short, fast and total victory. Seen from our present-day perspective, with armies in the West attempting to extract themselves from long-running and politically intractable conflicts, the Six-Day War remains especially compelling.

Even in the barest of outlines, the achievements and outcomes of the Six-Day War are profound. Between 5–10 June 1967, Israel's armed forces launched a pre-emptive attack against the combined (although not coordinated) forces of Egypt, Jordan and Syria in what was a three-front war, typically never a promising condition for victory. Despite being outnumbered, and potentially with the very survival of the Israeli state in question, the Israel Defense Forces (IDF) routed all their Arab opponents by air, land and sea in a matter of hours and days, profoundly expanding Israel's borders and defendable territory and changing the strategic map of the Middle East to this day. Although we can certainly say that the Six-Day War did not bring a victor's peace, it undeniably established the IDF as the world's most professional, innovative and competent military organization.

As the Six-Day War unfolded, international analysts and observers were watching it with more than mere interest in regional outcomes. For here, in microcosm, was a true Cold War confrontation playing out in the Sinai Desert, the Gaza Strip, the Golan Heights and on the West Bank, the opposing sides seeming to represent, through their weapons, tactics and, to a certain degree, doctrine, the wider opposition between the Soviet Union and the West. The Soviet Union/Eastern Bloc was the principal sponsor, supplier and advisor of the Arab states, while for Israel similar levels

of support were provided by the United States, France and Britain. Thus, if we look specifically at armour – the focus of this book – on the Egyptian side the main tank types were the T-34/85, the IS-3 heavy tank, the PT-76 amphibious tank and the T-54/55 (its finest bit of modern kit), all Soviet types. For the Syrians and Iraqis, the T-54 and T-34/85 armed many of its formations. On the opposing side, the core of the IDF armour was the US M48/M48A1 Patton and the M50/M51 Super Sherman (upgunned and modified Sherman tanks), the French AMX-13 light tank and the British Centurion (again, upgunned). On the basis of armour technology alone, at a superficial glance the Six-Day Way seemed to be a genuine superpower 'proxy war'.

As we burrow into the detail, however, the Soviet vs Western warfare model isn't quite clear cut. Jordan, for example, was tactically most influenced by its British and Western historical connections, including in terms of its armour types – it used the M47 Patton and also British Centurions. The waters are further muddied when we incorporate Syria's holdings of German World War II PzKpfw IVs and Sturmgeschütz III assault guns, and further still when we allow for each side's repurposing of captured tanks. And when it comes to tactical doctrine, the relationship between the Arab states and Israel and their external sponsors was never entirely aligned, for a range of cultural, political and military reasons that we shall explore below.

What the Six-Day War presented with clarity, however – and here the superpowers really did take note – was the outcome: the absolute superiority of Israeli forces over their opponents. The key take-home lesson was that a highly professional, superbly trained, technically competent and utterly motivated armoured force, one that could flexibly decentralize tactical initiative to the field commanders, would be able to outmanoeuvre, outfight and defeat an enemy with parity in technology, but which had poor standards of training, a lack of technical sophistication and inflexible and centralized command structures. That lesson had actually already been demonstrated to a large degree in the 1956 Arab–Israeli War. During this conflict, the IDF played

In the Sinai in 1956, Israeli clean-up and salvage crews remove destroyed armour, in this case an M4 Sherman. Note the penetration marks on the thin side armour, and the turret flipped upside down. The 1956 Arab–Israeli War built the IDF's confidence in the combat effectiveness of its Armoured Corps. (David Rubinger/The LIFE Images Collection via Getty Images)

In the aftermath of the 1956 battle in the Sinai, IDF tankers inspect captured Egyptian Shermans. Both sides used Shermans in this conflict, including the M1 and the M4 variant. (Bettman via Getty Images)

its part in the wider 'Suez Crisis' campaign, which saw Britain and France attempting to reassert control over the Suez Canal after its aggressive nationalization by the Egyptian President Gamal Abdel Nasser in his first year in office. During that brief conflict, the IDF soundly routed Egyptian forces in the Sinai, much as they would in 1967. But in the years between 1956 and 1967, the lessons of the 1956 war were mostly lost on Nasser, who explained the defeat away in terms of fighting a two-front war, and who saw future solutions principally in terms of quantitative build-up of men and materiel, courtesy of his new Soviet supplier. His lack of more nuanced awareness, plus an assortment of other errors on the part of the Arab armies, would bring disaster in 1967.

This book concentrates on a very specific, but crucial, part of the Six-Day War – the confrontation between Arab and Israeli armour. In part, it is undeniably the study of combat technology, as the conflict brought a variety of light, medium and main battle tanks into head-on combat. The design of armoured combat vehicles (ACVs) has always been a balancing act, and a trade-off, between three elements: mobility, armour and firepower. As any armour commander knows, you cannot have the best in all three, but rather weight the design towards the preferred elements. For example, you can give a vehicle heavy armour, but that in turn reduces its mobility, begging the question: Which is more important for survival –mobility or firepower? During the Six-Day War, these questions were tested in the most demanding and exposed of combat environments, and we will search for answers throughout. At the same time, however, the competence and professionalism of the crews meant that the vehicles on their own were not the only, and really not even the most important, arbiter of the battlefield outcomes. It is arguably possible that had the opposing sides swapped armoured vehicles completely, the Israeli victory would have been largely the same.

CHRONOLOGY

1955

IDF engineers fit Sherman hulls with the CN 75-50 turret, to create the M50 Super Sherman.

1956
29 October–
7 November

The Second Arab–Israeli War, or Suez Crisis; Israel defeats Egypt in the Sinai. Following the war, Egypt heavily rearms with Soviet tanks.

1959

British Centurion tank enters service with the IDF.

1964

Major-General Israel Tal takes command of the IDF Armoured Corps.

1965

The M51 Super Sherman, fitted with a 105mm gun, enters service.

1967
5 June

Six-Day War begins. The IDF launches Operation *Red Sheet* in the Sinai, with ground operations beginning at 0800hrs. At 1500hrs, the IDF also begins ground operations in the West Bank, as part of Operation *Whip*.

6 June

IDF armoured units make strong advances in the Sinai, albeit against very heavy resistance, with major tank engagements in the north and centre of the front. Ariel Sharon takes his division to victory at Abu Agheila. This day also sees a large-scale tank battle between the IDF and Jordanian armour in the Dothan Valley. By the end of the day, both Egyptian and Jordanian forces are in retreat.

7 June

IDF conquers Old Jerusalem. In the Sinai, the Giddi and Mitla passes are sealed, trapping much of the retreating Egyptian armour. The IDF also captures Jericho, and Jordan accepts a ceasefire.

8 June

The IDF conquers Hebron. Israel prepares for offensive operations against Syria in the Golan Heights.

9 June

At 0100hrs, IDF forces reach the Suez Canal. 1130hrs – Operation *Hammer*, the Israeli invasion of Syria, is launched, with fierce fighting on the Golan Heights. The 8th Armoured Brigade and 1st Golani Infantry Brigade manage to take key Syrian positions.

10 June

Syrian Army collapses. A ceasefire is agreed at 1830hrs, bringing the war to an end.

DESIGN AND DEVELOPMENT

Between 1948 (the year of the founding of Israel) and 1967, neither the Arab states nor Israel developed significant domestic production of armoured vehicles, particularly in terms of tanks. What tanks they did come to possess were either World War II surplus, colonial legacy vehicles or foreign imports, with local adaptations to varying degrees. This route of acquisition, rather evolutionary and haphazard in nature, goes some way to explaining the particularly broad spectrum of vehicles operated by the combatants. During the late 1950s and the 1960s, the situation was somewhat rationalized by a more focused relationship with suppliers, particularly on the Arab side. Egypt, Syria and Iraq in particular came to rely upon the Soviet Union as the chief provider of armour and associated equipment and doctrine, albeit not without some internal resistance within their armoured divisions. For the Israelis, the flow of armour from European and US suppliers was, it should be remembered, never an open tap – relations between Israel and the West were, as now, highly variable, and the West frequently exercised export caution according to the sensitivities and levels of tension in the Middle East. If anything, the achievements of the IDF's Armoured Corps are even more impressive when taking account of the wide-ranging types of vehicle it had to operate.

ISRAELI TANKS

The design and development story of Israel's tanks is essentially that of import and modification, rather than from-scratch production of new vehicles. The British

Centurion stands as a good opening model for this process. Development of the Centurion, a British tank, began in 1943. The programme was inspired by the need to compete with some of the heavier varieties of German armour, although production did not begin until January 1945 and its entry into service came just after war's end. In line with its original purpose, the Centurion was a true main battle tank (MBT), designed to slug it out at range with the heaviest of opposing armour.

The Centurion first entered service with the IDF in 1959, with the acquisition of the Mk 2 variant, followed by the Mk 3 and the Mk 5 and 5/1, all equipped with a 20-pdr gun and a Rolls-Royce Meteor 12-cylinder petrol engine. Initial fielding of the new tank brought disappointments for the Armoured Corps. The tank proved to be mechanically erratic in the desert environment, the litany of problems including engine overheating from dust-clogged radiators, poor control characteristics in some terrain (especially sandy slopes), burned-out brakes and even poor accuracy from the 20-pdr gun.

Two major shifts served to raise the Centurion in the eyes of the IDF. The first was that the Ordnance Corps invested in a programme of modifications to bring the Centurion up to new Israeli requirements. Much of this effort focused on upgrading the gunnery, specifically in swapping out the 20-pdr for the new British 105mm rifled L7 gun, which had entered production in the late 1950s on British Centurions and would go on to arm one of the finest British post-war tanks, the Chieftain. The L7

The Centurion Mk 3 (here a Canadian museum piece), along with the Mk 5, was adopted by the IDF. This vehicle is equipped with the Mk 3's original Royal Ordnance QF 20-pdr gun, but the IDF replaced most of these with the superior 105mm L7. Those tanks that retained the 20-pdr still had a potent weapon, one that could penetrate 305mm of rolled homogenous armour (RHA) with its AP shell. (Balcer/CC BY-SA 3.0)

Civilians wave to a unit of IDF Centurions, armed with the 105mm L7 gun, as they push into Syria in June 1967. The stowage boxes on the flanks of the turret are one of the distinguishing features of the Centurion; as well as providing convenient storage, they also gave additional 'stand-off' protection against HEAT shells. (© Hulton-Deutsch Collection/Corbis via Getty Images)

had largely been designed around defeating T-54 armour, hence it was a logical addition to the IDF Centurions, albeit one requiring substantial modification. Nevertheless, it gave the Centurion crew the ability to strike and destroy individual enemy tanks at 1,500m. Most of the IDF Centurions went into action in 1967 with the L7 fitted.

The second important step forward in Centurion capability came from procedural changes, not mechanical ones. In 1964, the Armored Corps was taken over by Major-General Israel Tal, a warrior whose combat experience stretched back to World War II and whose knowledge of all aspects of armoured warfare was unrivalled. Recognizing that some of the Centurion's problems were actually tied to human factors, Tal implemented a rigorous regime of training in maintenance procedures and gunnery, distributed strictly through the Centurion units. This work began to bear fruit in terms of Centurion reliability and also in the consistent accuracy of the long-range fire.

The L7-equipped Centurion in IDF service was known as the Sho't Meteor, 'sho't' being the Hebrew for 'whip'. The tank's two main positives were its newly acquired gun and its substantial armour (51–152mm), ticking the boxes of armour and firepower. With a loaded weight of more than 50 tonnes, however, it was never going to be particularly sprightly; it had reasonable acceleration, but its top speed maxed out at 34.6km/h, slow compared to the T-54 and most other Arab tanks. The IDF implemented a range of other modifications to the Centurions for their purposes.

Of older vintage than the Centurion, the US M4 Sherman was a long-term staple of

An AMX-13 tank on display at the Latrun Armoured Corps Museum in Israel. The AMX-13 began production in France in 1952, and imported vehicles served with the IDF in both the 1956 and 1967 wars. Here we have a good view of the FL-10 oscillating turret for the 75mm gun. (Katangais/CC BY-SA 3.0)

the IDF. In the earliest days of the Israeli state, war surplus Shermans from the North African and Italian campaigns were scrounged, acquired and bought from a hotchpotch of sources, the vehicles usually requiring impressive levels of repair, modernization and adaptation before they became fully functioning combat machines. For example, by 1950 the IDF 7th Armoured Brigade had a single Sherman tank battalion, but only two of the four companies were actually equipped with Shermans. Its A Company took M4s bought from a US Army weapons dump in Italy, but the vehicles were found to have had their guns stripped out. So, with some ingenuity, the IDF engineers managed to fit the Shermans with 75mm Krupp M1911 guns (found in a storage cave in Switzerland), marrying the gun with a 105mm howitzer loading mechanism (Eshel 1989, p. 24).

During the early 1950s, as their own problems with Arab unrest escalated in North Africa, the French became Israel's major supplier of Shermans, specifically M4A1s with the standard 76.2mm gun. Although the Sherman had been the foundation of American and British armour during World War II, its vulnerabilities against far superior German tanks such as the Tiger and Panther led to the stopgap development, by the British, of the Sherman Firefly, a standard Sherman modified to take the powerful Royal Ordnance QF 17-pdr gun. The IDF in the 1950s, faced with the new generations of Soviet armour, decided to implement a similar solution amongst its Shermans.

The gun chosen for the new tank was the French 75mm CN-75-50, as found on the AMX-13 light tank, another Israeli purchase from the French (see below). From 1954, Israeli engineers working at the Bourges Arsenal in France laboured to create a working marriage between the Sherman and the CN-75-50, a feat that proved to be intensely challenging, involving major adaptations to the Sherman's turret weight distribution, gun mantlet, internal space and loading mechanism. A developed

An M51 Super Sherman stands rusting, but still defiant, at the Harel Brigade memorial site at Radar Hill, Har Adar, Israel, formerly the site of an intensive battle on the West Bank between IDF and Jordanian armour. The M51 can be most easily distinguished from the M50 by its double-baffle muzzle brake. (Bukvoed/CC BY-SA 4.0)

prototype turret was finalized in 1955, and it thereafter went to Israel for fitting to the Sherman hull and to ready Israeli factories for production. The first 50 of the tanks utilized M4A4 hulls, powered by Continental R-975 gasoline engines and with a vertical volute spring suspension (VVSS) system. Subsequent trials showed that the extra weight of the tank was overloading both the engine and the suspension, so the eventual production models had more powerful Cummins V-8 diesel engines and more robust horizontal volute spring suspension (HVSS).

The M50 Super Sherman, as it is known, was ready in time to fight in the 1956 Sinai campaign. Although it certainly made a valuable addition to Israel's armoured punch there, the fighting capabilities of the tank raised some concerns during the late 1950s and 1960s. The 75mm gun had power limitations – or at least its ammunition did. During the Six-Day War, for example, it was found that the HEAT round could successfully penetrate the side armour of a T-54/55 at up to 2,000m, but the Soviet tank's front armour was impervious to such strikes. Thus, during the early 1960s, the IDF began exploring the possibility of upgunning the Sherman even further. Again, the French had a promising new weapon to offer the Israelis – the 105mm CN-105-F1, as fitted on the AMX-30 tank.

Convinced that the CN-105-F1 was the solution, the Israelis again set about adapting it for the Super Sherman. The two main issues were that the gun was simply too long to accommodate, and it was too powerful – there was not enough space inside the tank for the gun to recoil. So, the gun barrel was shortened substantially, by 1.5m, which dropped its muzzle velocity to 800m/s; a double-baffle muzzle brake was also fitted, one of the key outer distinguishing features from the M50. The tank was also fitted with a Cummins or Pratt & Whitney diesel engine and the HVSS suspension.

The M51 Super Sherman, also known as the Isherman, was ready in 1965, just in time to fight in the Six-Day War. Certainly, the IDF appeared to have maximized the potential for modifying the Sherman for modern warfare.

Another US tank, the M48 Patton was a 90mm-gun armed, four-man MBT that began its development in 1950 and which entered service in 1953. It became one of the most prolific of the American tanks, with more than 12,000 built. Israel had conducted long and arduous negotiations with the United States over the purchase of American armoured vehicles, particularly M47 Pattons (the predecessor of the M48). A cautious US administration shied away from direct supply, with two purchase requests turned down in 1955 and 1958, but in 1964 a sinewy solution was found. Wanting to supply the Israelis, but at the same time not wanting to annoy oil-producing Arab states, President Lyndon B. Johnson negotiated with the West German Chancellor Ludwig Erhard to supply Israel with 150 of West Germany's M48A2 tanks, as the Germans swapped them out for newer M48A3s. After predictable tensions and arguments, the deal was agreed and deliveries began shortly thereafter, the tanks actually moved to Israel by the Italian Army, the Germans keen to keep the arrangement at arm's length. Yet when just 40 machines had been shipped to Israel, word reached the outside world, causing an outcry that resulted in further German shipments ceasing. This obstacle finally spurred Johnson to overcome his reluctance, and the United States now permitted direct Israeli purchase of Pattons.

There is some confusion in historical sources about the exact variants of the Pattons supplied to the IDF by the United States. There were certainly the M48A2s already

delivered from Germany, plus US-supplied M48A1s and M48A2s. (The main differences between these two tanks related to fuel efficiency, engine performance and fire control.) Some sources claim that the United States also supplied M48A3s, as evidenced in photographs from the Six-Day War that have been unsuccessfully edited by the censor to remove all M48A3 identifying features. There is also the additional factor that some M48A2s were upgraded to M48A3 configurations in terms of powerplant, and small numbers even received L7 105mm guns as part of an armament upgrade. Getting to a final authoritative baseline source on this issue appears difficult. What we can best say is that the IDF before the Six-Day War was certainly equipped with M48, M48A1 and M48A2 Pattons, with the possibility of small numbers of M48A3s, either supplied by the United States or upgraded to M48A3 standards by the IDF.

The French AMX-13 light tank stood in contrast to the hefty Centurions, Pattons and Shermans. The first of these vehicles was purchased by Israel in the 1950s, and by 1967 the IDF had some 400 in stock, distributed between three battalions. The AMX-13 was firmly in the light tank category – it had a 75mm gun, a three-man crew (commander, gunner, driver), a loaded weight of just 15 tonnes, a maximum armour depth of 40mm and an overall length of 4.88m (hull). The most advantageous property of the AMX-13 for the IDF was its nimble nature, even over difficult terrain. In many ways, this simply reflected an earlier Israeli doctrinal investment in the principles of speed and manoeuvrability as key, before the new generations of Soviet armour changed the game more towards firepower and survivability. The AMX-13 also had a fast rate of fire from its auto-loader mechanism.

Super Sherman tanks push through the Sinai Desert at speed during the Six-Day War. Note the alternating direction of the gun barrels as they travel; like an elite infantry squad, each vehicle is covering a specific field of fire. (Photo 12/Universal Images Group via Getty Images)

AMX-13/75, 37TH ARMOURED BRIGADE, WEST BANK

The AMX-13 was the most vulnerable of the IDF tank types during the Six-Day War, on account of its very thin armour. On the hull sides and turret sides the armour depth was a mere 20mm, and the strongest parts of the tank – the hull front and turret front – were only double that, at 40mm. To compensate for its armour inadequacies, however, the AMX-13 was brisk on the move and manoeuvrable. Armed with the 75mm CN-75-50, if its crew intended to take on a heavy Arab tank such as a T-54/55 their best bet was to use the tank's speed to position itself to fire on the weaker side or rear armour; IDF AMX-13 tankers achieved several notable kills during the war in this way.

Crew:	3	Fording:	0.6m	
Weight loaded:	15,000kg	Gradient:	60 per cent	
Length o/a:	6.36m	Trench:	1.6m	
Length hull:	4.88m	Engine:	SOFAM Model 8 GXb 8-cylinder water-cooled petrol, 250bhp @ 3,200rpm	
Width:	2.5m			
Height:	2.3m	Armament:	1 × 90mm main gun; 1 × 7.62mm co-axial machine gun; 2 × 2 smoke dischargers	
Track width:	350mm			
Ground pressure:	0.76kg/cm²			
Max. road speed:	60km/h	Armour:	10–40mm	
Max. road range:	350/400km			

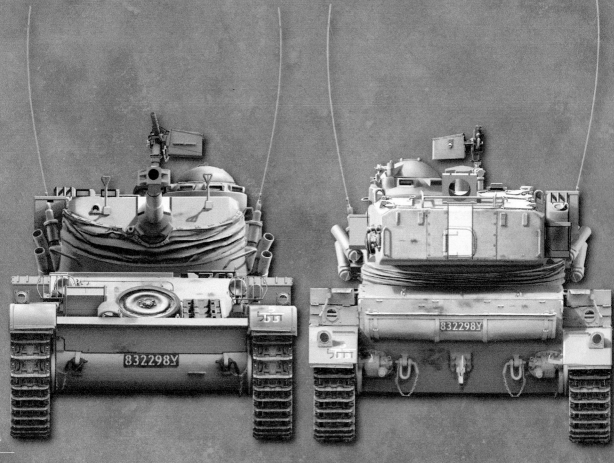

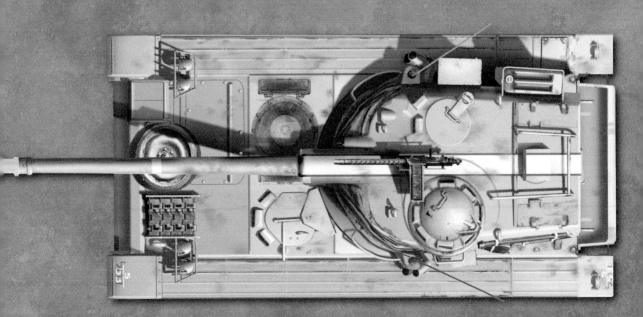

The AMX-13 was purchased and used largely unmodified. Its chief problem, however, was its extremely thin armour (see the illustration caption opposite), which, frankly, made it easy to kill, and its somewhat underpowered gun. The result was that quickly after the Six-Day War, most of the vehicles were sold off to Singapore.

ARAB TANKS

The composition of armour in the Arab states during the Six-Day War is a complex topic to compress, given the number of nations involved and the diversity of armour types, even with the progressively centralizing effect of Soviet-supplied armour during the 1950s and 1960s. To help make this picture a little more digestible, we will first note the armour types that were shared between Israel and their Arab opponents, before looking at the main Soviet vehicles plus the German panzers utilized by Syria.

It should be remembered that Israel's three primary foreign suppliers of armour – Britain, France and the United States – also had deep historical and sometimes ongoing military trade relations with the Arab states during the 1940s–60s. This meant that within all the Arab armies who fought in the Six-Day War, there were elements of European and American armour – in the case of Jordan these sources constituted the majority of its tanks. To take Centurions as our first example, in the early 1960s Britain sold some 90 Centurion Mk 5s to Jordan, these going to equip the Royal Guard Brigade and the 10th Tank Battalion. Unlike the IDF, the Jordanian

An M47 Patton on display at Latrun. One interesting point to note about the M47 was that it was the last US tank to be equipped with the bow-mounted hull machine gun, as seen here. The main user of the M47 Patton in the 1967 war was Jordan, which acquired 49 of the vehicles, equipping the 12th Independent Tank Battalion. (Oren Rozen/CC BY-SA 4.0)

Army did not upgrade their Centurions to the 105mm L7 gun, but retained the 20-pdr. Egypt also had some numbers of Centurions in its arsenal; a consignment of 64 were ordered in 1949 and delivered the following year. These were the earlier Mk 3s, which featured the 20-pdr gun and also a co-axial Polsten 20mm automatic cannon.

Looking to the United States, both M47 and M48 Pattons were supplied to Egypt. The former tank was slightly larger, longer and heavier than the latter, and, powered by a V-12 Continental Model AV-1790-5B, 7 or 7B that developed 810bhp @ 2,800rpm, marginally slower than the M48A3 but faster than the M48A1 and M48A2 in their original configurations. It was armed with the rifled 90mm M36 as opposed to the M48's M41 gun, but both weapons could fire the same ammunition types. The first deliveries of M47 Pattons to Jordan began in 1964, followed shortly by M48s and M48A1s, the total numbers received being 140 M47s and 160 M48/M48A1s. (Principal differences between the M48 and M48A1 were that the latter had a larger commander's turret hatch and fittings to mount a commander's .50-cal. M2HB machine gun.) The Pattons in Egyptian service remained with their 90mm guns, and did not receive any upgunning packages.

M4 Shermans – of assorted variants and modifications – also cropped up in Egyptian use, although by the time of the Six-Day War they were largely obsolete and few in number (many had been destroyed during the 1956 war). Most of the Egyptian Shermans came from World War II surplus, and over time the Egyptians did implement upgrades, improving engines and suspension and fitting some with the French 75mm CN-75-50, although by most accounts this modification was unsuccessful.

As we can see from this short profile, therefore, the armour clash of the Six-Day War was not simply a matter of Soviet vs Western armour; we could make the picture even more maze-like if we included armoured cars and armoured personnel carriers (APCs). But the factor that undeniably most influenced the armoured battle in 1967 was the injection of tanks provided by the Soviet Union during the 1950s and 1960s.

The T-34/85 was one of the most successful tanks of World War II, and the fact that it was manufactured until 1964 is testimony to its appreciable qualities. Designed,

Jordanian M48 Pattons gather near the border with Israel, just prior to the start of the Six-Day War. Note how the Browning M2HB machine gun on the turret is fitted with the conical flash hider; this was almost exclusively a feature of the tank-mounted machine guns. (Bettman via Getty Images)

A vintage Egyptian T-34/85, on display in Cairo. These vehicles were mainly acquired by Egypt from a Czech arms deal c. 1955, and the Syrians also began to acquire these vehicles direct from the Soviets in the early 1960s. (Francesco Gasparetti/ CC BY 2.0)

like the Centurion, in response to the appearance of the German Panther, the T-34/85 took the core advantages of the base vehicle – 60-degree sloped armour, very low ground pressure, excellent speed and cross-country mobility – and enhanced them with the fitting of the 85mm high-velocity gun.

Egypt received its first shipments of T-34/85s in 1956, acquiring them not from the Soviet Union but from communist Czechoslovakia's CKD factory, which licence-produced the T-34/85 and other Soviet vehicles, and later from the Skoda works. The advantage of purchasing from the Eastern Europeans was also that Czech standards of production were generally higher than those of the Soviets, and all the 820 Egyptian T-34/85s were new-build vehicles manufactured to high standards. Other enhancements included road wheels designed for the T-54, improved gearboxes and suspension, an enhanced gun breech block and better fire-control optics, plus more modern radio communications equipment (Benninghof 2019). Syria also received the new T-34/85s from Czechoslovakia in the late 1950s and early 1960s, and they came to form a significant element of both the Egyptian and Syrian arsenals.

Yet although the T-34/85 was an excellent tank in its heyday, by the time the Six-Day War arrived it was straining against outer limits of obsolescence, especially in terms of gunnery and survivability. As T-54s and T-55s arrived in larger numbers, the Egyptians confined them more to the organic tank battalions within regular infantry brigades (Benninghof 2019).

While the T-34/85 looked to the past, the T-54s and T-55s that entered Arab service in the 1960s were more firmly in the present (although its replacement, the T-62, had entered Soviet service in 1961). These tanks represented a fundamental leap forward in Soviet post-war tank design. Although they were fairly quickly superseded by more advanced variants – the T-62, T-64 and T-72 – the fact that up to 100,000 T-54/55s were produced and widely distributed by the early 1980s meant it was a core piece of kit for the Arab states during many Cold War conflicts, not least the Six-Day War, when it was the most advanced tank in Egyptian service.

The full design and development story of the T-54 and T-55 is a complex one, so here we will note only core characteristics. The T-54 was a development of the earlier T-44 medium tank, and it entered Soviet service by 1949. It was a four-crew machine with a noticeably low profile – disregarding its roof-mounted machine gun, it was only 2.4m high, giving it a challenging low silhouette for enemy tanks to spot and hit, especially in difficult terrain. The penalty, however, was that the interior was cramped for crew, gunnery and ammunition. In balance to these problems, the T-54 had very heavy armour (hence the IDF's racing investment in upgunning its own tanks), plenty of power, mobility and speed from its Model V-54 V-12 water-cooled diesel, and excellent fuel storage.

The T-55 entered production in 1958, and brought with it a whole gathering of improvements over the T-54 model. The profile was largely the same, but the vehicle now had full nuclear, biological, chemical (NBC) protection, an increased ammo load (45 shells, as opposed to 34 on the T-54), safer ammunition storage, a more powerful diesel engine, an increased fuel capacity (adding another 100km onto the road range), plus the improved 100mm D-10T2S main gun, with stabilization in both planes of movement.

The Egyptians operated both the T-54 and the T-55 tanks in the Six-Day War, largely without their own modifications or improvements. The tanks were again Czech productions, and the total orders were 350 T-54s in 1960 and 150 T-55s in 1963 (Benninghof 2019). The Syrians also received T-54s and T-55s from the same production works, and these went into the 14th and 44th Armoured brigades.

Under Nasser's rule, Egypt was an enthusiastic recipient of communist armour of many varieties, as it rearmed the nation following the 1956 war. In addition to the T-34/85 and T-54/55 mentioned above, some other distinctive types are worth noting. At the heavy end of the scale, the Egyptian Army acquired 100 SU-100 tank-destroyers and 100 IS-3 heavy tanks during a mid-1950s arms deal. Both of these vehicles were design relics of the Great Patriotic War. The SU-100 went into production in September 1944. It consisted essentially of a T-34 chassis fitted with a casemate superstructure and the 100mm D-10S gun that eventually went forwards into the initial versions of the T-54. The vehicle had reasonable armour (75mm max.) and performance (48km/h), and its gun could hold its own on the modern

This frontal view of an IS-3 tank gives an impression of its thunderous dimensions, its frontal armour some 200mm thick. Note the angled prow, which provided a further deflective feature. This frontal armour was relatively impervious to IDF tank guns up to and including the 90mm guns on the M48A2 Pattons. (Eddie Germino/ US Army Ordnance Museum/ Public Domain)

PT-76

The PT-76 was a light vehicle, weighing just 14 tonnes, and it was powered up to 44km/h by a Model V-6 6-cylinder inline water-cooled diesel that developed 240hp @ 1,800rpm. Mounted in the small top turret, home to the commander and gunner, was a D-56T 76.2mm gun, a development of the weapon first used in the T-34/76 tank. Although a light weapon by 1960s standards, it did have one particular virtue in a fast rate of fire, anywhere between 6–15rpm, although 6–8rpm was more common in combat. Its curse, however, was very light armour – just 14mm at maximum depth – meaning that it was very easy not only for enemy armoured vehicles to destroy, but also enemy infantry equipped with AT missiles. The PT-76 was fully amphibious, propelled via two hydro-jets mounted in the rear of the hull. A trim vane was fitted to the front of the hull just prior to entering water, while on land this was stored flat against the glacis plate. Max. speed on water was 10km/h.

Crew:	3	Max. road range:	260km
Weight loaded:	14,000kg	Fording:	Amphibious
Length o/a:	7.625m	Gradient:	70 per cent
Length hull:	6.91m	Trench:	2.8m
Width:	3.14m	Engine:	V-6 type 6-cylinder inline water-cooled
Height w/o AA MG:	2.225m		diesel, 240bhp @ 1,800rpm
Track width:	360mm	Armament:	1 × D-56T 76.2mm main gun; 1 ×
Ground pressure:	0.479kg/cm²		7.62mm SGMT MG
Max. road speed:	44km/h	Armour:	11–14mm

1. Hydro-jet pipe
2. Caterpillar track drive wheel
3. Engine transmission
4. Oil cooler
5. Powerplant
6. Water pump impeller
7. Fuel tank
8. Commander's station
9. Loader's station
10. D-56T 76.2mm main gun
11. Observation periscope
12. Ammunition stowage
13. Idler wheel
14. Driver's position
15. Fume extractor
16. Muzzle brake

A PzKpfw IV Ausf. H tank in a Spanish museum collection. Spain sold 17 of its 20 Panzer IVs to Syria, and this is one of the three vehicles that did not go abroad, therefore giving a solid impression of the Syrian tank configuration. (Contando Estralas/Museo de Unidades Acorazadas de El Goloso/ CC BY-SA 2.0)

battlefield. The main problem the SU-100 had when sent out to the Middle East was coping with the specific environmental conditions. Thus, the Egyptians upgraded the road wheels, suspension and gearboxes in much the same way as the T-34/85s had been improved.

The real monster in the Egyptian arsenal was the IS-3, lumbering in at 45.8 tonnes. The IS-3 began its development in 1944, the third in line of a series of World War II Soviet heavy tanks. Its two chief qualities were its survivability and the power of its gun. It had a prodigious armour depth (see *Technical Specifications*), making the tank difficult to destroy with anything other than the most powerful tank gun, and the 122mm D-25 gun was actually developed from a heavy Soviet field artillery piece, the M1931/37.

In Egyptian service, the IS-3 variant was the IS-3M. It had plenty of problems in Middle Eastern combat service, however. There were constant issues with the engine overheating under the tropical sun and its gunnery efficiency was poor: the tank's gun had two-piece ammunition, which resulted in a very slow rate of fire. These issues were compounded by the low profile (which, like the T-54/55, limited gun depression), the ability to store only 28 rounds on board and poor gunnery optics.

In 1956–57, Egypt also received 50 PT-76 amphibious light tanks. The first prototype of this vehicle was produced at the Kirov Plant in Leningrad/St Petersburg in 1950, with official production and adoption the following year. It was a striking piece of armour for the time, being fully amphibious, propelled through the water by two water jets in the rear of the hull, rather than the propeller or track propulsion adopted by many other countries. The PT-76 offered Egypt amphibious capability across waterways and along littoral waters, providing it with a degree more offensive flexibility. Syria also acquired small numbers of the tank, although more appeared in the later Yom Kippur War of 1973.

The PT-76 was not the most curious element of Syrian armour, however. During the 1950s Syria received respectable quantities of light armour (mainly Panhard

178B armoured cars) from France, which, making some efforts at impartiality, also provided armour to the Israelis, as we have seen. In the mid-1950s, France, alongside Spain and Czechoslovakia, offered the Syrians some 100 German wartime-vintage PzKpfw IV Ausf. H tanks, and also numbers of Sturmgeschütz III assault guns and some Panzerjäger IVs. The Panzer IVs had been stored well and reconditioned before sale, so they were in a good condition, but they were largely as they had emerged from World War II, with their Maybach gasoline engines and 75mm KwK 40 L/48 cannon. Although these tanks were certainly respected in World War II, and still had to be treated with respect by any opponent, they were undoubtedly showing their age by 1967, not least in their maximum speed (42km/h) and limited operational range of 200km. Still, as with several other vehicles in the Arab arsenal, they helped make up the numbers.

The tapestry of armoured vehicles that clashed in the Six-Day War means that this was a conflict with many layers of context and comparison. At one end of the scale, we have individual tank battles that looked almost reminiscent of engagements in Western Europe in 1944–45, while at the other we have clashes between some of the best and most developed armour on the world stage at that time. As is often the way in such engagements, the outcomes would be decided by a mix of the vehicles' technical capabilities and the skills of the tankers.

A captured Arab PT-76 tank in the Yad la-Shiryon Museum, Israel. This particular vehicle has the trim vane mounted on the front of the vehicle, to improve its performance through water. The gun is the D-56T with a double-baffle muzzle brake and fume extractor. (Uziel302/ CC BY-SA 3.0)

THE STRATEGIC SITUATION

OPPOSITE

This map shows the positions of the Egyptian and Israeli forces at the beginning of the Six-Day War on 5 June 1967, and the subsequent Israeli movements on each of the following days from 5–8 June, reaching the Suez Canal in the early hours of the morning on the 9th. It is apparent from this map that although there was an Egyptian armoured reserve held back around Bir Gifgafa, much of the Egyptian force was pushed into the eastern half of the Sinai, meaning that it was able to offer little defence in depth during an inevitable IDF counter-attack or, as it turned out, an Israeli offensive. Note also the position of Major-General Avraham Mandler's 8th Armoured Brigade in the far south, a deployment that served to pull key Egyptian formations away from the three-*ugdah* (division) thrust in the north.

Unpacking the strategic situation of the Six-Day War in Israel takes a little geographical and political imagination for those who live outside the Middle East (I am one of them). Despite its evident military superiority in the 1956 war, Israel remained geographically and demographically highly vulnerable to the Arab states around it, some of whom actively proclaimed that Israel had no right to exist. The country, on its pre-1967 borders, was roughly 400km long, but at its narrowest point was only 21km wide. The Jordanian-occupied West Bank bulged towards the Mediterranean, creating what to the tactically minded can only be called a salient, while the small Gaza Strip territory, at this time administered by Egypt, provided a vantage point for growing Palestinian insurgency. Egypt sat on Israel's entire south-western border, Jordan on most of the long eastern border and Syria to the north-east on the Golan Heights. To the far north was the Lebanon. In short, Israel was truly surrounded by its enemies.

The tension between Israel and its Arab neighbours was real and pressing, a powder keg with the fuse burning hot or smouldering angrily depending on mood and events. Between November 1964 and May 1967, for example, Israeli and Syrian armour and artillery regularly exchanged fire across the border during the 'War of Water', a clash over Arab intentions to divert the headwaters of the River Jordan that supplied arid Israel with much of its water. The Palestine Liberation Organization (PLO), formed in 1964, launched terrorist attacks into Israel from bases in Jordan, the West Bank, Lebanon, the Gaza Strip and Syria. Relations with the Jordanian government leaned towards tight-lipped accommodation, but Arab assassination

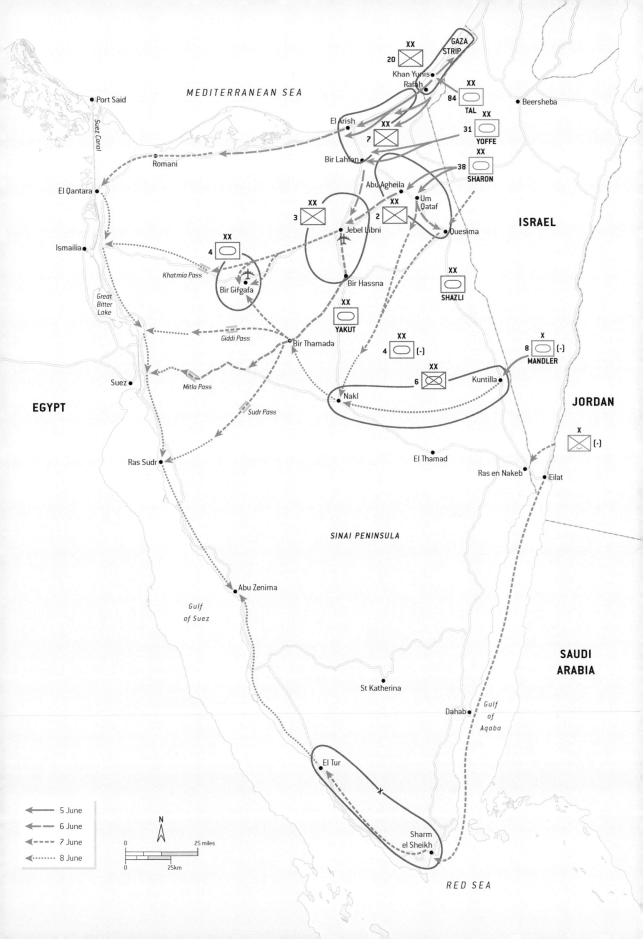

M48A1 Patton tanks pass the saluting base during a parade in Haifa on Israel's Independence Day. One feature separating the M48A1 from the M48A2 (also in IDF service) is that the former had five track return rollers, whereas the latter had only three. (Moshe Pridan/Public Domain)

attempts on King Hussein of Jordan questioned his long-term power. But most concerning of all to the Israelis was what was happening in their most powerful past and future enemy, Egypt.

Nasser's brand of expansionist Arab nationalism might, following the defeat in the Sinai in 1956, have stayed a mere defiant aspiration had it not been for the major rearmament programme in the late 1950s and first half of the 1960s, made possible by the Soviet injection of arms. It was this swelling of forces, combined with a reinterpretation of recent military history in Egypt's favour, that convinced Nasser that his country could take on Israel once again, this time with a victorious outcome.

Certainly, from the perspective of armour, the Arabs appeared to have the balance in their favour in 1967. By this time Israel had 1,294 tanks of all types, while Egypt alone had amassed an arsenal of 1,300 vehicles. Syria added another 750 tanks and Jordan 880. This meant that on paper Israel was faced with a combined armoured fleet of 2,330 Arab tanks, nearly double its own stocks. There were similar numerical disparities in aircraft and in infantry.

By the early to mid-1960s, Nasser's confidence was mounting, and it became increasingly clear that he was revving up to open conflict, with ever-more declarative speeches proclaimed over Radio Cairo. In November 1966, Syria and Egypt signed a defence pact, each promising to protect the other if attacked. Bearing in mind that cross-border clashes were frequent, this pact sent the signal to Israel that Egypt and Syria were essentially planning a two-front war.

Tanks, trucks and armoured cars gather in the Sinai Desert in May 1967, during the Egyptian build-up to war. The tanks appear mainly to be T-54/55s, suggested by the low profile and the distinctive egg-shaped turret, and possibly some assault guns. (Bettman via Getty Images)

The situation went up a gear on 14 May 1965, when Nasser suddenly began to deploy major infantry and armour formations into the Sinai. This move was followed just two days later by an ominous sign – Egyptian foreign minister Mahmoud Riad requested that the UN remove its United Nations Emergency Force (UNEF) stationed in the Sinai, a request that UN Security General U Thant acquiesced to on 18 May. The withdrawal came just a day after Syrian forces also began massing on the Golan Heights.

For Israel, the signs of an impending attack were becoming undeniable. There was a period of both nervous tension and political inaction within the Israeli government, but eventually, under the authority of a dynamic new defence minister, Moshe Dayan, it was decided that the IDF would opt for a pre-emptive attack. We should not see this decision as expeditionary aggression. Israel was geographically too small and narrow to think defensively, nor could its relatively small army of 264,000 men, many of them reservists whose civilian lives were integral to Israel's agriculture and economy, hope to fight a war of months' duration. Attack was quite simply the best form of defence.

The Egyptians also knew that attack was the IDF's best option. But here it made some critical mistakes in the way it deployed its armour and infantry. The classic Soviet model of defence was to create a defence-in-depth, drawing the attacker into multiple lines of resistance across a wide expanse of terrain, stretching his logistics to breaking point and inflicting attrition before the Soviet armoured formations counter-attacked at the decisive moment. This model, actually given a codename – *Kahir* – was the one subscribed to by many in the Egyptian high command, including General Abdul Mortagy, the commander-in-chief in the Sinai. However, Mortagy and others

On 1 June 1967, IDF Southern Command's Brigadier-General Ariel Sharon (centre) arrives by helicopter with generals Haim Bar-Lev (second left) and Yishayahu Gavish (second right) at an army base in the Negev Desert in southern Israel, just four days before the start of the Six-Day War. (David Rubinger/GPO via Getty Images)

were overridden at the last minute by Nasser, who insisted on deploying the bulk of his forces close up to the Egyptian–Israeli border, a fatal strategic move. By forward deploying most of his troops and armour, albeit with some armoured reserves in the centre of the front, it meant that if the Israelis could punch through this crust, they would be able to encircle, outflank and trap the Egyptian formations, who had nothing but miles of burning desert to retreat into.

In terms of the actual deployments on the eve of the Six-Day War, the Egyptians had a total of seven divisions in the Sinai on 4 June 1967. They had built strong positions, defensive rings of minefields, anti-tank weapons, infantry fighting positions and armour groups, with heavy artillery support. From north to south they were as follows:

- 20th (Palestine) Infantry Division – This division occupied the Gaza Strip. It was augmented with some 50 Shermans.
- 7th Infantry Division – Deployed between El Arish and Rafa, just beneath the Gaza Strip, its responsibilities included the narrow Jiradi Defile. Its force included 100 tanks, a mix of T34/85s and IS-3s.
- 2nd Infantry Division – This division, with *c.* 100 T-34/85s and T-54s in support, occupied the area around the key junction at Abu Agheila, just over 40km in from the coast and a commanding position for any forces attempting to make an east–west transit.
- 3rd Infantry Division – Also with *c.* 100 T-34/85s and T-54s, the 3rd Infantry Division sat to the east of the 2nd Infantry Division deployed on the Jebel Libni–Bir Hassna line in central Sinai.

- 4th Armoured Division – This was one of the most potent Egyptian armoured formations, with some 200 T-55s. It was positioned just to the east of the 3rd Infantry Division around Bir Gifgafa, and was intended to make a massive armoured counter-attack on Israeli formations.
- Task Force Shazli – Led by Major-General Saad el Din Shazli, this armoured unit had 150 T-55s and sat near the Israeli border to the south-east of Bir Hassna, and was intended to punch into Israel, advancing through the Negev Desert and cutting off Eilat.
- 6th Mechanized Division – Shielding the El Kuntilla–Nakl east–west axis, the 6th Mechanized Division was in the far south of the front.

The Israeli forces facing the Egyptians consisted of three armoured divisions (*ugdah*) and an independent armoured brigade, the major units commanded by General Israel Tal, Major-General Avraham Yoffe, Brigadier-General Ariel Sharon and Major-General Avraham Albert Mandler. Tal's division, which included the 7th Armoured Brigade (66 Pattons and 58 Centurions) and 60th Armoured Brigade (52 Shermans and 34 AMX-13s) was in the far north opposite Rafah and off the southerly tip of the Gaza Strip. Next down was Yoffe's division, which had a total of 200 Centurions in the 200th and 520th Armoured brigades. Sharon's division, positioned opposite Abu Agheila, included the 14th Armoured Brigade (56 Centurions and 66 upgunned Shermans) and the 99th Infantry Brigade (allocated 28 Shermans). Mandler's division, in the far south opposite El Kuntilla, included the 8th Armoured Brigade, which had 50 Shermans.

In the broadest of outlines, Tal's, Yoffe's, Sharon's and Mandler's formations were to thrust into the Sinai along their respective axes, driving through the Egyptian defences, capturing the Khatmia, Giddi, Mitla and Sudr passes in the west, and reaching the Suez Canal, inflicting an imperious defeat on the Egyptians in the process. On the other fronts, the composition of forces and the objectives were quite different. For the West Bank, the main Israeli armoured unit deployed for the assault upon Jordanian-held Jerusalem was the 10th Mechanized Brigade equipped with Shermans, while in Samaria the 45th Mechanized Brigade would lock horns with the Jordanian 25th Brigade and, more significantly, with the 40th Armoured Brigade with M48 Pattons.

To the north, along the Golan Heights, Syria was to deploy nine brigades, including two armoured and one mechanized, although each of the six infantry brigades also included an armoured battalion with *c.* 40 T-34/85 or T-54 tanks in each. The tanks took up their positions within an imposing network of fortified mountain positions, each of the three main routes winding up the Golan Heights covered by numerous strongpoints and firing positions. To face this precipitous and well-defended objective, IDF Northern Command (Major-General David Elazar) would mainly rely upon the 1st Golani Infantry Brigade, which included Sherman support, and the 8th Armoured Brigade (during the war the 8th Armoured was reassigned to Northern Command). It was a formidable objective for such a lean force against a well-prepared enemy.

So it was that as dawn rose on 5 June 1967, the IDF launched one of the most audacious offensives in modern military history. For them, there was no palatable alternative to outright victory.

TECHNICAL SPECIFICATIONS

To balance both depth and scope of coverage, in this section we will focus purely on the more modern vehicles that formed the bulk of the IDF and Arab armour during the Six-Day War.

ISRAELI TANKS

CENTURION SHO'T METEOR

The Centurion Sho't Meteor was a four-man tank, consisting of the commander, driver, gunner and loader. The power-operated cast turret held three of the four men – everyone apart from the driver. The commander sat at the top of the tank to the right of the gun, with a vision cupola that featured a 10× magnification periscope with 360-degree rotation; this meant that he could have all-round vision while remaining under armour. The gunner sat below and in front of the commander, operating a periscopic sight with a ballistic-pattern graticule, while the loader was on the left of the gun. Note that in addition to his loading duties, the loader also acted as radio operator, co-axial machine-gunner and managed the Mk II smoke discharger. (There were two banks of smoke dischargers, one bank of six launchers each side of the turret.) The driver sat down in the front hull, separated from the rest of the crew by a covered hatch. He operated the vehicle via (left to right) clutch, brake and accelerator pedals and two steering levels that altered the speed of the tracks. An ammunition stowage bin was to his left.

An Israeli 105mm-armed Centurion advances into the Sinai on 7 June 1967. The photograph captures the intense dust thrown up from the desert floor by the tracks, a material that caused severe mechanical difficulties for the Israeli Centurions on first adoption, but which was largely alleviated by tighter maintenance practices. (Ullstein bild via Getty Images)

The engine compartment at the rear of the vehicle housed a Rolls-Royce Meteor Mk IVB 12-cylinder liquid-cooled petrol engine that developed 650bhp @ 2,250rpm. The tank weighed more than 50 tonnes, however, so this engine could only push the vehicle to a maximum road speed of 34.6km/h, relatively pedestrian by the standards of main battle tanks of the time. It also had a comparatively heavy ground pressure for the time ($0.9kg/cm^2$), which could make handling tricky on loose and sandy ground. The transmission gearbox was a Merritt-Brown Z51R, featuring five forward and two reverse gears. For safety, the engine compartment was separated from the fighting compartment by a fireproof bulkhead. The Centurion ran on petrol, 458L of which were stored at the rear of the vehicle. This gave the Centurion a quite poor road range of 102km, dramatically less than the T-54 and T-55, and which contributed to a long chain of fuel logistics behind Sho't battalions.

The armament of the Sho't was, as noted above, either the original 20-pdr (83.4mm) gun or the upgraded 105mm L7. In the original British Mk 5, the armament package was completed by 7.62×54mm co-axial and turret-mounted AA machine guns, the former initially the BESA and the latter the Browning M1919. In Israeli service, it was common to see the AA gun replaced with a .50-cal. Browning M2HB. This not only enabled the commander to lay down heavy suppressive fire, should he need to, but the ballistic properties of the .50 BMG cartridge also gave it a secondary role as a ranging weapon.

M50/M51 SUPER SHERMAN

The M50/M51 Super Shermans, like the M4 Sherman they were derived from, were both five-man tanks. Two drivers/gunners occupied the forward hull positions, the

CENTURION MK 5 SHO'T METEOR, 10TH 'HAREL' ARMOURED BRIGADE, SINAI FRONT

The Centurion Mk 5's standard armament was the same 20-pdr gun that equipped the Mk 3, but the Mk 5/2 variant was issued with the 105mm L7 gun. The two guns can be distinguished by the configuration of the fume extractor on the barrel: the 20-pdr's fume extractor was centralized around the barrel with fins on top, while the L7's fume extractor had no fins and was set in a slightly asymmetric relationship to the barrel. This tank's 20-pdr has been upgraded to the 105mm L7, as were most of the Centurions in the IDF by the beginning of the Six-Day War. Note the unit markings on the barrel and the hull. The white chevron marking on the hull armour skirt indicates which company the tank belongs to: V indicates the tank is in the 1st Company; > indicates the 2nd Company; ^ indicates the 3rd Company; < indicates the 4th Company. The barrel rings do not indicate 'kills', but rather the battalion to which the tank belongs: one ring indicates the 1st Battalion, two rings the 2nd Battalion, and so on.

Crew:	4		Gradient:	60 per cent
Weight loaded:	50,728kg		Trench:	3.352m
Length o/a:	9.85m		Engine:	Rolls-Royce Meteor Mk IVB 12-cylinder
Length hull:	7.56m			liquid-cooled petrol, 650bhp @
Width:	3.39m			2,250rpm
Height w/o AA MG:	2.94m		Armament:	1 × 105mm L7 main gun; 1 × .30-cal.
Track width:	610mm			(7.62mm) co-axial MG; 1 × .50-cal.
Ground pressure:	0.9kg/cm^2			(12.7mm) AA gun; 2 × 6 smoke
Max. road speed:	34.6km/h			dischargers
Max. road range:	102km		Armour:	51–152mm
Fording:	1.45m			

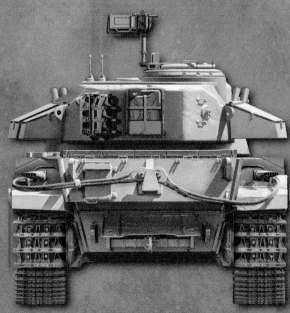

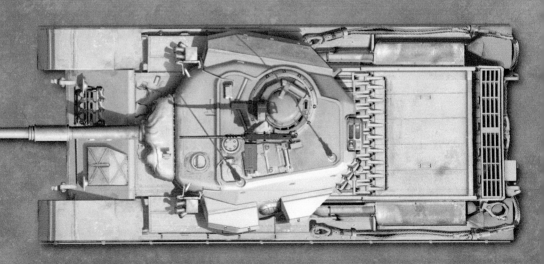

A close-up view of the HVSS fitted to the M50 and M51 Super Sherman. The mechanism was essentially a version of the British Horstmann suspension, but replaced the Horstmann's coil spring with a pair of volute springs. (Bukvoed/CC BY 3.0)

primary driver on the left and the hull machine-gunner/assistant driver to his right, while the commander, loader and gunner were in the turret up above. The Sherman ancestry meant that many of the performance characteristics were similar to those of the original American tank, depending on which variant of the Sherman provided the hull. Basic performance characteristics of the M4A3 Sherman were a top speed of 42km/h, a range of 161km (on 636L of fuel), a ground pressure of 0.924kg/cm^2 and a fording capability of 0.914m. The M50 and M51, through their modifications, improved on these statistics to varying degrees, taking the range up to more than 250km and the top speed up to 45km/h. Attempts also seem to have been made in the Isherman to reduce the ground pressure; while some M51s had the standard Sherman 419mm track width, others were subsequently fitted with wider 584mm tracks.

As stated above, the big difference between the Super Shermans and the original vehicles related to gunnery and powerplant. Regarding the latter, the standard Sherman powerplant for an M4A4 was the 20.5L Chrysler A57 multibank petrol engine, which generated 370hp @ 2,400rpm. The M50 received the Continental R-975 (a licence-built version of the Wright R-975 Whirlwind), which substantially upped the power to beyond 400bhp, and later the Cummins VT8-460 V-8 diesel, developing 460hp @ 2,600rpm. The M51 also had the Cummins engine, giving the two tanks similar performance characteristics. Backing up the powerplant was the shift to the HVSS suspension system, which gave better holding characteristics over loose and difficult ground. In the preceding VVSS, the suspension consisted of cone-shaped springs (volute springs), whose spring coils slid over each other during compression to make for a very compact and effective suspension unit. The superior HVSS worked by springing a pair of dual-mounted road wheels on each bogie with a horizontally mounted volute spring. This system meant that when the volute springs were compressed by either the front or the rear bogie wheel-arm, the pressure was applied to the opposite arm, which helped to keep tension smoothly and consistently maintained on the tracks. The HVSS also had distinct maintenance benefits, including being easier to change individual road wheels.

The critical change between the baseline Shermans and the M50/M51 was the gun systems. Fitted to the M50, the French 75mm CN-75-50 was a modified version of the German 7.5cm KwK 42 L/70, which equipped the Panther and the Jagdpanzer IV self-propelled anti-tank gun. The French gun delivered a muzzle velocity of more than 900m/s, which stood in impressive contrast to the Sherman's 600m/s with its standard gun.

The M51's 105mm CN-105-F1 was an even more potent piece. It was a 56-calibre gun matched with a revolutionary new form of HEAT ammunition, manufactured by DEFA. HEAT ammunition performs best when fired from smoothbore guns, as the gyro-stabilized spin imparted by rifled barrels weakens the delivery of the molten metal penetrating jet on impact. But gyro-stabilization improved gunnery range, accuracy and muzzle velocity. The French solution was a unique HEAT shell, which consisted of an inner shell and an outer shell, the two separated by ball bearings. When the shell was fired, the outer shell was rotated by the rifling, spinning on the ball bearings, while the inner shell carrying the HEAT warhead stayed still. Muzzle velocity was in the region of 1,000m/s.

M48 PATTON

As explained previously, the M48 Patton tanks used by the IDF were principally the M48, M48A1 and M48A2 variants, with the possibility of some M48A3s also in action.

We can note the commonalities between the vehicles. All are four-man vehicles, with the driver seated in the hull and the commander, loader and gunner in the turret. In the M48A1 and M48A2 variants, the commander had the M1 cupola, fitted with an M28 sight and vision blocks, and capable of 360-degree traverse. The gunner worked his trade via a ×8 periscope and a telescope of the same magnification. The

M48A2

Crew:	4	Gradient:	60 per cent
Weight loaded:	47,173kg	Trench:	2.59m
Length o/a:	8.729m	Engine:	1 × Continental AV-1790-8 12-cylinder
Length hull:	6.87m		air-cooled engine developing 825bhp @
Width:	3.631m		2,800rpm
Height o/a:	3.13m	Armament:	1 × 90mm M41 main gun; 1 × .30-cal.
Track width:	711mm		(7.62mm) co-axial machine gun; 1 ×
Ground pressure:	0.83kg/cm²		.50-cal. (12.7mm) M2HB AA machine
Max. road speed:	48km/h		gun
Max. road range:	258/402km	Armour:	12–120mm
Fording:	1.219m		

M51 SUPER SHERMAN, 14TH 'ZIPPORI' ARMORED BRIGADE, SINAI FRONT

This M51 Sherman of the 14th Armoured Brigade (commanded by Colonel Mordechai Zippori) is seen in its early configuration, with a single storage box on the side of the tank (later versions display two boxes). Other features on the side of the vehicle include spare track links, two spare road wheels and extra jerry cans of fuel. One of the key distinguishing features of the M51 from the M50 is the distinctive double-baffle muzzle brake at the end of the 105mm CN-105-F1 gun, this being fitted to minimize the recoil of the powerful gun within the turret space, by diverting some of the muzzle gas to the side and to the rear. The white band painted along the top of the vehicle is an air recognition marking, designed to give Israeli Air Force (IAF) pilots a quick way to distinguish friend from foe, although not all IDF vehicles display this marking in the Six-Day War.

Crew:	5	Max. road range:	270km
Weight loaded:	39,000kg	Fording:	1.07m
Length o/a:	n/a	Gradient:	60 per cent
Length hull:	6.05m	Trench:	2.44m
Width:	2.62m	Engine:	Cummins VT8-460 V-8 diesel, developing
Height w/o AA MG:	2.75m		460hp @ 2,600rpm
Track width:	419mm (standard)	Armament:	1 × 105mm CN-105-F1; 1 × .50-cal.
Ground pressure:	0.927kg/cm^2		(12.7mm) AA gun; 2 × 7.62mm
Max. road speed:	45km/h		(7.62mm) MGs (hull and co-axial)

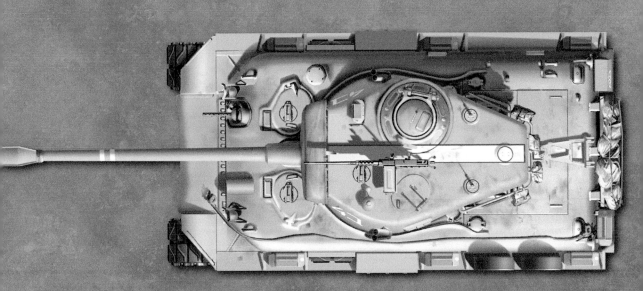

loader had a stock of either 60 (M48/M48A1), 64 (M48A2) or 62 (M43A3) 90mm shells to draw upon.

By 1960, the Patton had reached the M48A3 variant, which had a loaded weight of 47,173kg, a ground pressure of 0.83kg/cm^2 and a maximum road speed of 48.2km/h from the improved Continental 12-cylinder AV-1790-2A, which developed 750bhp @ 2,400rpm. These performance figures were actually little different from the previous variants. What had changed, and significantly, was the range. Maximum range was an impressive 463km; the previous variant, the M48A2, had a maximum range of between 258 and 402km (Foss 1979, p. 100).

The tank's main armament was the 90mm M41 gun, fitted to a turret with full powered traverse and elevation (one complete turret rotation could be performed in 15 seconds). Foss notes that 'The turret system is electro/hydraulic with manual controls for use in an emergency, and the commander can override the gunner if required' (Foss 1976, p. 101). This latter function was especially important; tank commanders often had better visual acquisition of the surrounding battlespace, and had to be able to respond to either threats or target opportunities briskly.

AMX-13

The AMX-13 was a diminutive vehicle powered by a SOFAM Model 8 GXb 8-cylinder water-cooled petrol engine that developed 250bhp @ 3,200rpm. Given the 15-tonne weight of the tank, the engine could propel the vehicle to a maximum road speed of 60km/h, and with a ground pressure of 0.76kg/cm^2 it had generally good handling over loose or soft terrain. Its major downside was naturally its light armour; a hit from any tank shell usually meant game over for the vehicle and usually its crew.

The AMX-13's gun was the 75mm CN-75-50, firing HE and HEAT ammunition. It was fitted into an unusual FL-10 oscillating turret, with elevation achieved by tilting the entire upper part of the turret; traverse came from rotating the entire turret. This design, as well as facilitating improved depression and elevation, also allowed fitment

This photograph illustrates the considerable height difference between the M50 Super Sherman in the foreground and the AMX-13 stood next to it. The M50 was created with a variety of Sherman hull types; this vehicle appears to have one of the larger hulls, likely an M4A3. (Oren Rozen/ CC BY-SA 3.0)

of an autoloader, feeding from two six-round magazines on either side of the turret bustle (a total of 37 rounds were carried). This meant that the AMX-13 could engage targets quickly with multiple shots, although once the magazines were emptied, the crew had to reload the magazines from outside the vehicle. (The AMX-13's specifications are provided in the colour illustration commentary.)

ARAB TANKS

T-34/85

The T-34/85 had a five-man crew – commander, gunner, loader, driver and hull gunner – the last two occupying hull positions while the others were positioned around the turret. For the commander, a post-war improvement included a traversable cupola; previous versions had been fixed. Turret traverse could be either powered or manual. The tank had a height of 2.743m, giving it roughly the same height silhouette as the Patton, although it was significantly narrower at 2.997m. From a construction point of view, the T-34/85's chief virtue was its well-sloped armour, although by the mid-1960s neither the slope (60 degrees on the glacis plate) and certainly not the armour depth (90mm) gave any advantages against the modern generations of tank guns.

Several design elements gave the T-34/85 continuing utility, despite its age. It had wide tracks – 500mm – for a tank of relatively low weight (32,000kg loaded), meaning that it delivered decent cross-country performance. It had a brisk road speed of up to 55km/h (speed was the key to its survivability), courtesy of a V-2-34m V-12 diesel engine, and a useful range of 300km, which could be extended through the fitting of external fuel drums.

The gun on the T-34/85 was the ZIS-S53 85mm gun, which was developed from the M1939 anti-aircraft gun. Trained by the gunner using a TSh-15 sight, the weapon was still to be respected: a high-velocity armour-piercing (HVAP) shell from the gun could penetrate 130mm of armour at 1,000m. Its chief disadvantages were nevertheless also related to gunnery, its systems being unsophisticated by the standards of the time, plus the low survivability if struck by 90mm or 105mm shells.

A disabled Syrian T-34/85. By this point in history, the T-34/85 was largely obsolete, and the tanks were mainly used in static defensive positions, which made them very vulnerable to IDF tank gunnery and to IAF air strikes. Although the Syrian tank positions on the Golan Heights often gave cover against direct fire from the ground, they could be more exposed to CAS strikes from the air. (Vittoriano Rastelli/ Corbis via Getty Images)

T-34/85

Crew:	5	Fording:	1.32m
Weight loaded:	32,000kg	Gradient:	60 per cent
Length o/a:	8.076m	Trench:	2.5m
Length hull:	6.19m	Engine:	1 × V-2-34 V-12 water-cooled diesel,
Width:	2.997m		500bhp @ 1,800rpm
Height w/o AA MG:	2.743m	Armament:	1 × 85mm ZIS-S53 main gun;
Track width:	500mm		1 × .30-cal. (7.62mm) DTM co-axial MG;
Ground pressure:	0.83kg/cm²		1 × .30-cal. (7.62mm) DTM bow MG
Max. road speed:	55km/h	Armour:	18–90mm
Max. road range:	300km		

T-54 AND T-55

Both the T-54 and T-55 were four-man vehicles – commander, loader, gunner and driver. They were encased in a highly protective steel shell (an all-welded hull and a one-piece cast turret), with some impressive armour depths: 70mm on the hull upper side, 100mm at 60 degrees on the glacis plate and 170mm on the mantlet. The T-55 added the security of a full NBC kit, denoted most visibly by the disappearance of the turret-mounted dome ventilator and the loader's cupola, both features on the T-54.

The T-54 and T-55 were substantial vehicles, with a fully loaded weight of 36,000kg. Nevertheless, they had respectable speed and manoeuvrability, with a road speed of 48km/h (T-54) or 50km/h (T-55) and good acceleration; the power-to-weight ratio of the T-55 was 16.11hp/ton. The T-55's fuel capacity of 900L (the T-54 had 812L) was also useful in the open desert operations, as the T-54 had a range of 400km while the T-55 took that figure up to 500km. The tanks could also be fitted with schnorkel devices to extend the fording depth to 5.486m.

This collection of former Egyptian Army T-54/55s were photographed in Gaza after the Six-Day War. More than 100 Egyptian tanks were captured by Israel during the conflict, and some were put into service within the IDF. In addition to T-54s and T-55s, the IDF repurposed Arab Centurions, M47 and M48 Pattons, and IS-3 heavy tanks. (Morse Collection/Gado/Getty Images)

The big issue with these tanks, already alluded to, was their low height profile, just 2.4m. This enhanced their survivability in terms of silhouette, but the low turret ceiling resulted in limited gun depression, meaning that they struggled to fight from a protected hull-down position, and in the cramped conditions the rate of fire was a worryingly low 3rpm. The main gun, however – the powerful 100mm D-10TG (T-54) and D-10T2S (T-55) – was impressively capable of destroying any IDF tank. A HEAT projectile, for example, was capable of penetrating 380mm of armour at 1,000m. But the internal ammunition capacity of the T-54 was just 34 rounds, only 11 of which were stored as 'ready rounds'. A Centurion, by contrast, could carry more than 60 shells.

The interior of an East German T-55 tank, viewed through a cutaway in the hull. This image shows the physical limitations of space inside the turret, with much of the interior taken up by the breech of the 100mm D-102TS gun. (JustSomePics/CC BY-SA 4.0)

IS-3

The IS-3 was a mighty four-man tank, with an overall loaded weight of 46,800kg, much of that weight coming from its prodigious armour: from 20mm of floor armour, the depths then escalated up through 120mm at 55 degrees on the glacis and an impressive 200mm on the gun mantlet. The weight translated, however, into unimpressive performance figures – a max. speed of 37km/h and a range of just 150km, running from a fuel capacity of 520L. It was powered by a V-2-IS (V2K) V-12 water-cooled diesel, which developed 520hp @ 2,000rpm.

The IS-3's main gun was the D-25T M1943 122mm weapon, with a vertical sliding breech block and a double-baffle muzzle brake. It could deliver an armour-piercing high-explosive (APHE) shell weighing 25kg out to ranges of 900m and still penetrate 160mm of armour. That weapon, combined with its very low profile, of just 2.45m, and heavy armour, were the pillars of its survivability, but some of the problems of its gunnery have already been noted. Another limitation was its absence of an infrared driving system as fitted on the T-54 and T-55; the Arab armies in general would struggle especially when engaging the Israelis in night actions.

IS-3

Crew:	4	Fording:	1.3m
Weight loaded:	45,800kg	Gradient:	60 per cent
Length o/a:	9.725m	Trench:	2.5m
Length hull:	6.77mm	Engine:	V-2-IS (V2K) V-12 water-cooled diesel,
Width:	3.07m		520hp @ 2,000rpm
Height w/o AA MG:	2.44m	Armament:	1 × 122mm D-25T main gun; 1 × .30-cal.
Track width:	650mm		(7.62mm) DTM co-axial MG; 1 × .50-cal.
Ground pressure:	0.83kg/cm²		(12.7mm) DShK turret-mounted MG
Max. road speed:	37km/h	Armour:	20–200mm
Max. road range:	150km		

T-54A, EGYPTIAN ARMY, SINAI FRONT

The profiles of this Egyptian T-54A immediately give a sense of the tank's relatively shallow silhouette, although this is raised somewhat by the addition of the turret-mounted DShkM machine gun. Another recognizable design feature is the egg-shaped turret, which held the commander, gunner and loader in rather cramped conditions. The T-54 and T-55 both had torsion bar-type suspension with five road wheels, the gap between the first and second road wheels being another identifying feature. One important distinction between the two related to gun stabilization. The D-10TG gun on the T-54A was stabilized in the vertical plane only, whereas the weapon on the T-55 was stabilized in both the vertical and the horizontal planes, making it a more accurate piece to use on the move.

Crew:	4	Fording:	5.486m (with schnorkel)
Weight loaded:	36,000kg	Gradient:	60 per cent
Length o/a:	9m	Trench:	2.7m
Length hull:	6.45m	Engine:	1 × V-54 V-12 water-cooled diesel,
Width:	3.27m		520bhp @ 2,000rpm
Height w/o AA MG:	2.4m	Armament:	1 × 100mm D-10TG main gun; 1 ×
Track width:	580mm		7.62mm co-axial MG; 1 × 12.7mm turret-
Ground pressure:	0.81kg/cm²		mounted AA MG
Max. road speed:	48km/h	Armour:	20–170mm
Max. road range:	400km		

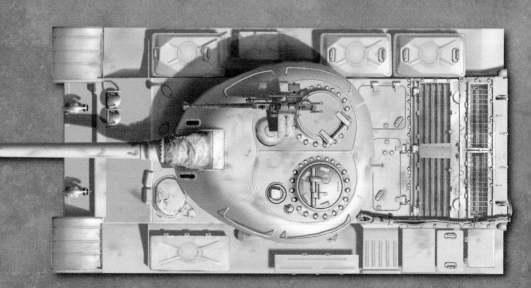

IS-3 TANK, 122MM AMMUNITION

Here are the principal ordnance types used by the IS-3 tank, fitted with the D-25T gun, during the Six-Day War. The 122mm weapon was the most potent of all the tank guns on the Sinai battlefield in 1967, although the capabilities of the weapon were let down by the slow reloading rates resulting from the two-piece ammunition.

A. Cartridge

The D-25T gun used two-piece ammunition, the propellant cartridge loaded separately to the shell itself. Here we see the cartridge type used with high-velocity shells.

B. VOF-471N

The VOF-471N round (projectile type OF-471N) is a Frag-HE type weighing 25.53kg and filled with 4.85kg of cast TNT explosive. This shell type was used against personnel and static material targets, but it could also damage or destroy armoured vehicles, particularly lighter types or if striking thin side or rear armour.

C. Cartridge

E. The 122mm cartridge for the VBR-417 and VBR-417B shells.

D. VBR-471B

The VBR-471B (with projectile BR-771B) is an armour-piercing – tracer (AP-T) round, used specifically for anti-armour work. The weight of the complete round is 39.32kg and the weight of the projectile, as fired, is 25kg. The explosive filler of the projectile is an RDX/aluminium mix, and the total weight of this filler is 0.156kg.

E. VBR-471

The VBR-471 is actually a variant of the VBR-471B. It essentially has the same projectile, but with a pointed nose and no windshield. The windshield, also called a ballistic cap, is designed to improve a shell's aerodynamic performance; it disintegrates on impact without having any effect on the penetration process.

A   B   C   D   E

THE COMBATANTS

An article in the November 1971 edition of *Military Review* entitled 'Israeli Armor: Lessons from the Six-Day War' confidently provides the primary reason for the IDF's armoured supremacy on every front in 1967:

> The most important ingredient of the Israeli victory with armour was the quality and efficiency of their tank crews. They won essentially because each individual was more effective in combat, especially in regard to accuracy of fire. A 75-millimeter, medium-velocity round that hits its target is better than either a 100-millimeter, high-velocity solid shot or a 122-millimeter shell which misses. Israeli tank superiority was due, in part, to the nature of the individual members. (Weller 1971, p. 45)

This statement deserves some unpacking. The calibre references in Jac Weller's text clearly hint towards the practical inferiority of T-54/55 and IS-3 tanks when faced by superior IDF crews, even when the Israelis were armed with lighter tanks and weapons. What we will not see in the combat description below is an utterly one-sided battle during the Six-Day War; the Israelis often had to fight hard for their gains, and they suffered some moments of serious setback and took heavy losses. Yet it seems undeniable that the outcome of the war was to a large, indeed *major*, degree due to Israeli competence, professionalism and training, traits that ran up through the entire command structure. In comparison, the Arab forces, while brave and in parts highly professional, went into battle critically hobbled by inadequacies in command-and-control, doctrine and overall training, issues that were quickly exposed as the Israelis took the initiative.

THE IDF

We should take a moment to set the IDF's Armoured Corps of the 1960s within wider Israeli military culture, for armour was just part of a collective whole that fostered similar values and approaches. Israel was a country militarized, out of brutal necessity, from top to bottom. It had forged a true 'citizen army' of *c*. 260,000 personnel, with a small rump of professional soldiers to which were added conscripts (there was universal military conscription), but the majority – three-quarters of the Israeli Army – were reservists, typically aged between their early 20s and 50 years old. In many armies around the world, the notion of a reservist often suggests inactivity and, potentially, amateurism. Because of Israel's constant operational demands, however, the IDF's reservists were true warriors, committing a month of every year to military training and frequently finding themselves on active deployment. Unlike most other armies, furthermore, a significant percentage of the Israeli troops were combat veterans; reservists in their 40s might have fought in two or three major wars by 1967. Furthermore, as Weller argues, the general upbringing of many Israeli youths could be a military induction in itself:

> What is near unique, however, is the fact that many of these lads learned all there was to know about the weapons and mechanical equipment in their kibbutzim before their national service ever began. They were well grounded in general education also, and had some paramilitary training which, in some cases, included combat. Less than 25 percent of Israeli youths have been exposed to the type of life encountered in the 'settlements,' but virtually all have some preinduction training. (Ibid., p. 45)

It was certainly the case that simply growing up in Israel during the 1940s–60s inculcated a background military education, which contributed towards an effective

This photograph, one of a famous set of images, shows a formation of Israeli Centurions, all mounted with 105mm guns, standing in the Negev Desert in readiness for crossing the Israeli border into the Sinai. Note how each man has an Uzi submachine gun, compact personal firepower that was perfect for storing inside an armoured vehicle. (Government Press Office (Israel)/

MAJOR-GENERAL ISRAEL TAL

Few figures have had an equivalent or greater impact on the development of the IDF than Major-General Israel 'Talik' Tal. Born in Zephath (Safed) in 1924 and raised in Moshav Be'er Tuvia in the British Mandate of Palestine, the young Tal joined the Jewish Brigade at the age of 17 during World War II, fighting as a machine-gunner in the Italian campaign. Returning to Israel after the war, he joined the Haganah (a Jewish paramilitary organization) then, following Israel's independence, became an infantry platoon commander, fighting in the 1948 Arab–Israeli War. During the 1950s, Tal developed an expertise in armoured warfare, and following his command of the 10th Infantry Brigade in the 1956 war he moved over to the Armoured Corps, taking command of it in 1964. Tal revolutionized IDF armoured tactics during this period, demonstrated by the superb tank-led manoeuvre warfare in the Six-Day War. The 1967 war was the high point of Tal's military career.

During the 1973 Yom Kippur War, however, when he was deputy chief of staff, Tal fell out with much of the IDF high command over tactical decisions, and he retired from the army the following year. Working in the Defence Ministry,

however, Tal did a final service to IDF armour as the leading figure in the design of the Merkava tank, which entered service in the 1980s. Tal died in September 2010, following a decade of ill health after a stroke in 1999.

Just prior to the onset of hostilities in 1967, Israel Tal (right) consults with Colonel Raful Eitan, commander of the 35th Brigade (Paratroopers Brigade). The relationship between the IDF Armoured Corps and airborne forces was a close one, the paratroopers providing the tanks with elite infantry support. (Government Press Office (Israel)/CC BY-SA 3.0)

professionalism when channelled into formal military service. We must not take this argument too far – after all, many Arab men were equally familiar with experience of war. But for the IDF this experience combined with a moral urgency – Israelis would fight, quite literally, for their country's survival – plus a general excellence in training.

IDF armour training had had a rather evolutionary history. The Armour School had been founded at Ramleh in 1949, led by a former British Royal Tank Regiment (RTR) soldier, Warrant Officer Desmond Rutledge, and whose trainers and training manuals were international, often speaking different languages. Eshel notes that in this potentially chaotic training environment, the trainees were compelled to learn their craft in an intensely hands-on way, experimenting constantly with gunnery, driving, maintenance and manoeuvre, and solving problems as they arose. This approach not only bred a deep familiarity with the vehicles, but it 'enabled the recruits to develop original ideas, concepts and tactics which later developed into one of the world's finest armoured techniques' (Eshel 1989, p. 25). During the 1950s, the IDF did inject some more formal approaches into the Armour School, based on experience gained by Israeli officers in foreign training programmes, but the fundamental attitude of innovation and independence never left the IDF armour crews.

A sea change in IDF armour training came with Major-General Israel Tal's leadership of the Armoured Corps from 1964 (although there had certainly been

many innovations before this point). Tal, an armour man through and through, brought an intense and unrelenting competitive professionalism to IDF tank training and tactics. Every aspect of armour operations came under scrutiny and the efficiency of procedures was refined, with a strict eye for individual and unit discipline. A critical object of his focus, however, was gunnery. All tankers received ever-more demanding gunnery training, the objective being to increase the rate of first-round hits at long ranges to as close to 100 per cent as possible. Tal wanted his gunners to be able to strike targets at beyond 1.5km, and motivated his crews to achieve such goals through high-stakes competitive events and constant gunnery practice: the IDF tankers firing ten practice shells for, on average, every individual round fired by the Arab armoured units. This was a tactically canny move, as from experience Arab armour crews tended to hold their fire until just a few hundred metres off their targets; Tal was aiming to claim the battlefield at long range by turning his gunners into the armoured version of snipers.

The IDF tankers who went into action in 1967 were therefore a genuine elite, and there was an extremely high esprit de corps extending across the chain of command. The four- or five-man tank crews developed especially strong bonds of brotherhood between them; armour conscripts could spend a total of 30 months in each other's company, achieving the most intuitive level of understanding of each other and of their vehicles and weapons. As with gunnery, the IDF tankers would also have

An Israeli tank moves into the Gaza Strip. The problems of dust obscuration are evident in this picture. Not only did it interfere with manoeuvre and gunnery, but the dust could also provide a convenient target indicator for the enemy, being visible from kilometres away on a clear day. The photographer, Paul Schutzer, was killed shortly after this picture was taken, when the half-track he was travelling in was hit by an Egyptian artillery shell. (Paul Schutzer/The LIFE Picture Collection via Getty Images)

Jubilantly waving from the turret of their tank, an IDF armour crew celebrates the complete IDF victory on 10 June 1967. Note the way in which personal kit is hung from the rear turret rail, there being little storage space inside the vehicle itself. (Vittoriano Rastelli/Corbis via Getty Images)

hundreds of miles of training missions under their belts, including operations alongside infantry and air units – combined-arms training was introduced in earnest in the 1950s, and would pay dividends in 1967, although the psychological dash of the armour could strain the bonds of the working relationship with infantry at times.

In action, IDF armour was known for its offensive aggression, operational tempo and tactical flexibility. Much of this was derived from its quite decentralized approach to command. There was a respected chain of command, and units would certainly hold fast to achieving mission orders, often at great personal cost. But discipline was generally bought by competent, inspirational leadership, not by mere position. The close questioning of the logic of orders by subordinates was common, and in battle, when communications might be cut or erratic, commanders at all levels were given implicit permission to act personally in relation to opportunities or threats, as long as they still kept orientated on the overall mission.

A portrait of Brigadier-General Ariel Sharon. By the Six-Day War, Sharon had already gained a vast amount of front-line combat experience, and was known for the aggression and dynamism of his leadership, although most of his previous wartime command experience was in charge of infantry. (Universal History Archive/Universal Images Group via Getty Images)

This attitude, and the fact that even leaders at brigade level would often lead their units directly into battle, frequently produced highly individualistic armour commanders, true mavericks playing at the very edges of discipline. Probably the greatest example of this character is that of Brigadier-General Ariel 'Arik' Sharon, a man known for his brutal battlefield drives that literally crafted a campaign on the move. Israel Tal himself would be seen at the head of brigade columns during action. Even at the level of armour battalions, companies, platoon and even individual tanks, the IDF armour crews were meant to demonstrate informed innovation. They also placed a premium upon relentless movement; frequently they would drive through enemy positions at speed with their guns blazing, shooting up every target before punching through and continuing out the other side towards a distant objective, leaving some enemy positions or forces intact, but reeling, behind them.

One further element that aided the IDF's dynamic combat efficiency was its organizational structure. The major formation structure of IDF armour was the brigade. In times of war, brigades might be formed into *ugdah*, which are divisional in scale but in concept and composition are more akin to battlegroups or task forces, formed with a specific operational objective in mind. Looking specifically at armour brigades, these were composed of three tank battalions, a reconnaissance company and supporting artillery (typically 120mm mortars transported in APCs), plus supply and administration units. The battalion then divided down into three companies, of three platoons per company. By the time of the Six-Day War, the IDF armour company consisted of 11 tanks, reduced considerably from previous years, when the company might have had as many as 17 tanks. This was a sensible policy, for it meant that in the confusion of battle it was far easier for a platoon commander to keep control of all the vehicles in his unit, thus enabling more coordinated manoeuvre, better speeds and tighter concentrations of fire.

ARAB FORCES

The multi-front defeat of the Arab armies in the Six-Day War was, to a large degree, an outcome related to fundamental structural, cultural and command relationships at the heart of the Arab armies, including within the armoured forces. We must naturally resist, however, the instinct to generalize and tar all the Arab states and units with the same brush.

Jordan, for example, had one of the most professional militaries in the Middle East, albeit a relatively small one. Until March 1946, Jordan had been the British mandate of Trans-Jordan under which, in 1920, the British-led Arab Legion was formed. This formation would endure beyond Jordanian independence until 1956 when, following the Arab defeat against Israel, the Legion was transformed into the Royal Jordanian Army. Up to this point, Jordan's army had been guided by British military expertise and leadership, and most of its officers were imbued with British attitudes towards professionalism and competence. (This went right to the top – King Abdullah had served with the British Army in World War II and his successor, King Hussein, from 1952 had attended the Royal Military Academy Sandhurst.) In the Jordanian armoured force, this resulted in high standards of training, vehicle maintenance and gunnery. Such standards were weakened a little from 1956, when all British personnel were expelled from the army, but they persisted enough in 1967 to make the Jordanian armoured units serious peer enemies for the Israelis.

The same could not be said for Syrian forces. The Syrian Army entered the Six-Day War with a significant level of combat knowledge amongst its commanders and armour crews, having been involved in various Middle Eastern struggles since the 1948 Israeli War of Independence. It had *c.* 550 tanks in its arsenal in 1967, although as we have seen these were a mixed bag of types, including those of World War II vintage. Historically, however, Syria had struggled to implement combined-arms operations, particularly in terms of the cooperation between artillery and armour, despite efforts to do so. The Syrian Army was also affected by the volatile internal politics of the country, and the disruptions of outside influences. By February 1966, the country had experienced a total of nine coups since 1945, one of them occurring just a year prior to the Six-Day War. This political fluidity affected continuity of command and control, even though military elements were often behind many of the coups.

The largest of the Arab combatants in 1967 was Egypt. The country had some strong traditions of military professionalism, but following Nasser's coup in 1952 the nation's senior commanders spent a large portion of their time wrapped up in political intrigues, rather than enhancing the preparedness of the armed forces. Egyptian armoured forces, though potent in scale and equipment, also suffered from a set of cultural and political conditions that hampered their effectiveness. Many of these elements can be applied more generally to the Arab armies.

Photographed in the 1950s, King Hussein of Jordan poses on a tank with army troops. The neat uniform standards hint at the professionalism of the Jordanian forces. IDF crews would often display a lax attitude towards uniform codes, seemingly without any impact on their unit discipline. (Loomis Dean/The LIFE Picture Collection via Getty Images)

FIELD MARSHAL ABDEL HAKIM AMER

In the aftermath of the Arab defeat in the Six-Day War, Abdel Hakim Amer took the lion's share of blame for the defeat of Egypt in the Sinai campaign. Born in 1919, he brought to the war long military experience, graduating from Cairo Military Academy in 1938, the following year receiving his commission into the Egyptian Army. Amer was subsequently at both military and political front lines. He served in the 1948 Arab–Israeli War and participated in the military coup that overthrew King Farouk in 1952. His actions in bringing Nasser to power served him well – in 1953 he was made the Egyptian Chief of Staff (jumping four military ranks in the process) and in 1956 he was appointed commander-in-chief of a joint Egyptian and Syrian military command. In the same year he commanded Egyptian forces during the 1956 Suez War.

Amer's downfall came with Egypt's devastating defeat in the Six-Day War. His order to retreat in the Sinai after the Battle of Abu Agheila made him a direct target for blame, and he was relieved of all duties on 17 June. The following August, Amer was arrested along with many others for allegedly plotting to overthrow Nasser, and on 13 September, while under house arrest, he apparently committed suicide by swallowing large amounts of pills, although much evidence points to his murder or forced suicide.

Gamal Abdel Nasser (on the sofa, far left) sits alongside the members of the Military Revolutionary Council after Egypt was declared a republic in June 1953. Second to his right is Abdel Hakim Amer, the man often regarded as a key figure responsible for the defeat of Egypt in the Six-Day War. (Keystone/Hulton Archive/Getty Images)

The core problem related to military education and a highly stratified command and control system. The overwhelming focus of military training at this time was largely 'rote memorization' (Pollack 2019, p. 439) of basic military skills and formulaic tactics, increasingly based on Soviet tactical models that were not always readily applicable to the Middle Eastern theatre. This is not to say that Egyptian forces did not understand modern combined-arms operations and manoeuvre warfare, just that they largely modelled these tactics in limited and unimaginative set-piece scenarios, with little ability to adapt them in the saddle according to evolving events. This problem was made worse by three other factors. First, Egyptian military society was culturally hierarchical; front-line initiative by individual commanders or crews was largely not part of the tactical mindset, and deviation from formulaic plans was frowned upon. This resulted in a sluggish and fragile command structure, one that could be easily outpaced by the more free-wheeling and adaptable Israeli armoured forces. Second, levels of education amongst the armour crews and army in general were low; only 9 per cent of army personnel had high school diplomas, and there were problematic levels of illiteracy. The lack of education limited the technical skills and tactical intuition of many Egyptian armour crews. Quantifying the significance of this factor is difficult, but the evidence from many tank vs tank engagements in the Six-Day War shows that in most such clashes, even when the IDF was outnumbered, the Israeli tank crews would generally and quickly take the ascendancy, inflicting

An IS-3 heavy tank rumbles past dignitaries in Cairo on 20 June 1956. Note the spare track links on the front hull. In all tank armies during the war, track links might be positioned around the hull and turret to provide a modicum of extra protection against anti-tank shell penetration. (AFP PHOTO FILES/ AFP via Getty Images)

disproportionate losses on their enemies. The lack of technical expertise also affected rates of vehicle maintenance and repair – on the eve of battle an estimated 45 per cent of Arab tanks fell short of being fully operational – while in battle there were problems operating unfamiliar Soviet-supplied radio sets and gunnery equipment.

A third factor was the paucity of relevant training for Egyptian armour crews in the years and months leading up to the Six-Day War. Gunnery practice was extremely limited, with some crews going into the 1967 war having fired only a few dozen rounds on the range, and at unrealistic targets. There was almost no investment in combined-arms training, despite the Minister of Defence, General Mohamed Fawzi, having overseen the production of a detailed training report advocating and detailing such training (the report was endorsed by Amer, but no action taken on its principles). As such, Fawzi has noted that in the training years 1965 and 1966, no Egyptian tanks practised gunnery in combined armour and infantry exercises. Shockingly, only 11 per cent of the total fuel allocated to armour training was consumed in the same period.

Compounding this failure was a general Egyptian focus on defensive actions rather than offensive manoeuvres; the result was an undertrained armour force lacking offensive dynamism. The belief that recent Egyptian combat experience in the Yemen was adequate to the challenge of combat against the Israelis in the Sinai was also fatally misplaced, as the two theatres were utterly different. Fawzi points to the fact that the 141st Armoured Division was pulled from the Yemen and only reached its sector in the Sinai on 4 June 1967, going into battle the very next day without any acclimatization.

The final factor in our consideration of Egyptian forces is the involvement of Soviet advisors and the supply of Soviet equipment from the 1950s. The Soviet Union imported a set of doctrines and training principles that were not always a ready fit for the Middle Eastern theatre, nor was the advice of Soviet advisors often appreciated by Egyptian commanders. Mohamed Heikal, the journalist who had a close relationship with Nasser himself, noted some of the key issues regarding the authority of the Soviet advice:

> Was the advice given by the experts indeed only advice, or had it to be acted on? When a ruling was given that the advice was, in fact binding on them, many officers felt humiliated. They did not feel that Egypt's defeat [in 1967] was due to any deficiencies on their part that foreign experts, again with their inevitable interpreters, were likely to be able to put right. After all, they had combat experience and their advisors had not. They had commanded tanks and flown MiGs against the enemy, which the Russians had not. They knew local conditions in a way that their advisors never could. Russian military thought was still conditioned by memories of World War Two's 2,000-mile front, whereas the Egyptian army was never likely to operate on a front of more than 100 miles (the length of the Suez Canal). Moreover, the quality of the experts varied considerably [and while some] commanded universal respect ... others were less admirable and, as the proverb says, sickness is contagious but health is not. (Heikal 1976, pp. 181–82)

Notably, the suspicion amongst Arab troops and their Soviet advisors was not merely one-directional. Interviews conducted with high-ranking Soviet advisors in the second half of the 1960s showed that many Russians were also highly sceptical of Arab responsiveness to innovation, technical instruction and tactical flexibility.

Taking all the factors together, it is clear that the Egyptian and Arab armour crews would be labouring on the battlefield under a heavy set of limitations that did not affect the IDF tankers. The results of this imbalance would become clearly and painfully revealed for the Arab armies in just six days of fighting.

Syrian T-54s on parade in Damascus, with Nasser in attendance. The military cooperation between Syria and Egypt was largely poor and often ill-tempered. These are early-model T-54s, indicated by the complete lack of fume extractor on the gun; this was introduced in the T-54A variant. (Keystone-France/Gamma-Keystone via Getty Images)

COMBAT

SINAI FRONT

The Israeli campaign in the Sinai – Operation *Red Sheet* – hung squarely upon the movement and firepower of IDF armour. Israel Tal, whose offensive in the far north of the theatre would be tactically critical, delivered the following stirring words to his crews just before the assault began at 0815hrs on 5 June:

> We shall be the first formation to open the assault … Our division has the best brigades in the army and we are expected to succeed. If we fail, the outcome will be disastrous for the whole campaign. There will be heavy fire and Egyptians will fight well, so keep moving. If you stall the attack, you will be subjected to tons of steel coming on top of you; therefore keep moving under all circumstances and fire from as far as possible, knocking out the enemy tanks and anti-tank guns at long-range. (Quoted in Eshel 1989, pp. 63–64)

Tal's ultimate objective was to break through enemy defences in the southern Gaza Strip around Khan Yunis, and then drive to the east following the coast road to seize the important and also heavily defended Rafah Junction, before heading on to Jiradi and El Arish. The M48A2 Pattons and the Centurions of the 7th Armoured Brigade (Colonel Gonen) began the attack with the strike at Khan Yunis, one that quickly slowed down under very intensive enemy fire. Gonen therefore sent the Pattons of the 79th Tank Battalion on an outflanking manoeuvre to the south.

Tank vs tank combat was quick in coming, with the IDF Pattons and Centurions facing Egyptian IS-3s, T-54s and T-34/85s, often at close quarters. The IDF gunners

quickly demonstrated that they could outfight the Egyptian armour, however, and by midday most of the enemy tanks around Khan Yunis had been neutralized.

Tal's division developed its advance through multiple separate lines of attack, throwing the Egyptian response into confusion. The advance on Rafah ran in two lines, the 79th Tank Battalion on a northern axis while the 82nd Tank Battalion made its push deeper to the south in an outflanking action, although this movement took it through slower and more difficult terrain. The enemy resistance around Rafah Camp (a refugee camp established in 1949) and Rafah Junction was stiff, but Tal's exhortations to keep the momentum going were respected, especially by a two-company reserve Centurion force commanded by Lieutenant-Colonel 'Pinko' Harel. Swinging his armour deep to the south, he managed to smash through enemy defensive positions and drove his tanks to the west. Here Harel himself recounts something of the experience, including encounters with enemy armour:

My orders were to take the two Centurion 105mm companies of 82nd Tank Battalion and to strike west towards Rafah Camp. Racing around the outer minefield, I made straight for the camp and started to engage enemy tanks at long range. The Egyptians were now under full alert and covered my approach with heavy artillery and mortar fire. Overhead I saw some Fouga trainers, turned into makeshift fighter bombers, swooping into the fray, firing rockets onto the enemy positions ahead. Moving slowly south, to outflank the outer enemy positions, I received order to go at top speed to Rafah Junction where Ori's recce company was in trouble. This was what I was waiting for! Ordering my

In this astonishing photograph, the scale of the Egyptian defeat in the Sinai is conveyed by hundreds of destroyed Egyptian vehicles, their blackened remains snaking through the Mitla Pass. The vehicles were largely destroyed by relentless IAF air strikes, plus tank gunfire. (David Rubinger/Government Press Office (Israel)/CC BY-SA 4.0)

IDF CENTURION VS EGYPTIAN T-54A, SINAI DESERT, 7 JUNE 1967

North of Bir Hassna on 6 June 1967, an IDF Centurion of Yoffe's division engages and destroys an Egyptian T-54A. We are viewing the enemy tank, which is at a distance of about 500m, through the Gunner's Primary Sight (GPS) slaved to the L7A1 rifled gun, which had a maximum firing range of 4,000m and a maximum rate of fire of 10rpm. The Centurion gunner is targeting the weaker side armour of the T-54A, which was 79mm thick on the hull upper sides and 20mm on the hull lower

side, although 130mm on the turret sides. This view also gives a good impression of the low profile of the T-54A, which was one of its greatest assets in terms of survivability. This IDF gunner, however, achieves a clean first-round hit with an M156 high-explosive squash head tracer (HESH-T) shell. A HESH warhead works by squashing its plastic explosive filling as a 'pat' against the tank armour before detonation; the resulting compression shock wave causes pieces of metal, known as 'spall', to be detached at high velocity from the interior of the armour, inflicting casualties and materiel damage inside the vehicle.

tanks into line, we charged straight ahead into the enemy position, crashing through their lines with main guns and machine guns blazing! To our right were some friendly Pattons engaged in a sharp battle with dug-in T-34s. After our crazy race through enemy fire we reached the high ground and took stock. All my tanks seemed intact, although two or three were smoking badly. Many had lost their bazooka plates. Behind us and below, dozens of enemy tanks were flaming hulls, their crews running frantically in shock and horror. But now I saw my chance to do some real tank fighting. To my right there seemed to be the objective as given to 7th Armoured Brigade. Rallying my two companies and after a quick orders group, we set off at top speed before the enemy could recover their senses and realise what we were up to. But not for long! As my spearhead, Capt. Aaron, climbed up the desert track leading to the road, the entire front exploded with fire. Tanks, anti-tank guns and mortars were firing. The first three Centurions got through safely, but the fourth exploded in flames. I shouted to continue the race and my tanks followed me through the curtain of fire – and we made it! (Quoted in Dunstan 2009, p. 46)

Harel's breakthrough was crucial to the development of the battle in the north. He took his Centurions on through the Jiradi Defile, a narrow stretch of coastal terrain that was massively defended with artillery, minefields, anti-tank guns and also 36 Egyptian Sherman tanks, fitted with AMX-13 turrets. The IDF Centurions battered their way through with speed, firepower and bravado, firing constantly with every weapon, the Egyptians stunned by the audacity and violence of the attack. Having made it through, the IDF force reached El Arish by mid-afternoon, low on both ammunition and fuel, the other Israeli tank units still east of the Jiradi Defile, which the Egyptians had now firmly closed behind Harel's armour.

For the Egyptian tank crews, these first few hours of the Six-Day War had been chaotic. They had lost many tanks in rapid order, not only to IDF armour but also to air strikes and artillery. They were also losing the tactical initiative, having particular trouble developing a coordinated response between the divisions. Localized Arab counter-attacks were swiftly stopped or repelled. For example, ten IS-3 tanks, an armoured reserve of the 11th Infantry Brigade, were pushed into the fighting around Rafah, but IDF Pattons wiped them all out, the first kills coming at a range of 1,000m.

For Tal, it was imperative that Harel's advance unit was reinforced and resupplied. To do so, the 7th Armoured Brigade made further fast, punishing runs through the Jiradi Defile and surrounding defences, the battle going on into the night hours with infantry also performing critical clearance actions at close quarters. By the early hours of 6 June, Harel had received reinforcements, fuel and ammunition, and they quickly replenished for the fight ahead.

An Israeli armoured unit advances across the Sinai. One of the biggest problems faced by the IDF tanks during this campaign was outrunning their supply lines, especially as the Israeli doctrine of a fast and deep offensive penetration meant that armoured vehicles could reach forward positions while leaving the territory behind unsecured for soft-skinned vehicles. (Keystone/Stringer/Getty Images)

The Israeli capture of El Arish led General Mortagy to issue orders for an immediate counter-attack by the 4th Armoured Division, positioned to the south with several hundred modern T-54s and T-55s. But their intentions would be foiled by the progress of Yoffe's division westwards. Since the launch of the invasion it had been grinding forward through the sand dunes of the Sinai interior. Despite the slow going, it managed to reach Bir Lahfan, which sat astride an important track junction just to the south of El Arish. There it took up positions as a blocking force against the Egyptian armour coming up from the south.

At around 2300hrs on 5 June, the T-54s and T-55s approached Bir Lahfan, unaware of what waited in front of them. The Centurions opened up with their main guns in a strobe-like display of night-time gunnery, hitting tank after tank with 105mm shells. The Egyptian force, even though it outnumbered the Israeli unit significantly, stopped and traded shells at distance, a contest in which they came off the worst. By mid-morning, with further IDF advances coming in from the east and tanks being hit by air strikes, the survivors of the 4th Armoured Division did an about-turn and headed back towards Jebel Libni in the south.

While Tal and Yoffe were engaged to the north, Sharon's division was making its own dynamic contribution to the war. Sharon's objective was to attack and clear the Um Qataf (Um Katef)–Abu Agheila area. This area was heavily defended to a depth of 35km, the nature of the terrain to the north and the south meaning that it could not be outflanked. As well as trenches, anti-tank guns, minefields and plentiful artillery, the Egyptians here also had the support of dug-in T-34/85s and T-54s plus 88 T-34/85s and SU-100s attacking as an armoured reserve. Altogether the Egyptians could bring 200 tanks against Sharon's assault.

The plan to crack this tough nut has been recounted by Sharon himself in his autobiography *Warrior*; from this, it is worth recounting his thinking in sequential detail, as it enables us to see the intelligent integration of IDF armour with infantry, airborne units and artillery in an efficient combined-arms operation. Sharon envisaged a closely coordinated attack on the Egyptian infantry defences, tanks and artillery

Tanks from Tal's division in the Sinai crest the top of a sand dune and take up protective positions as half-track-mounted infantry move up. The deep track marks cut into the sand illustrate why the terrain slowed the Israeli advance at several points along the front. (Public Domain)

An IDF light observation aircraft overflies a column of Israeli infantry half-tracks during the Six-Day War. Mechanized infantry were an integral part of each Israeli armoured brigade, but their open-topped vehicles proved to be highly vulnerable to artillery fire. (Moshe Milner/Government Press Office (Israel)/ CC BY-SA 4.0)

from the north, west (behind Abu Agheila) and east (a frontal attack), with each attack securing the flank of the neighbouring force. Following a deception attack against Quesima (Kusseima) with a brigade under Uri Baidatz, Sharon would then 'isolate the battlefield'. In the southern sector, a screening force of armour and mortars under Arie Amit would prevent enemy reinforcements deploying from Quesima and would provide a lodgement for attack in that direction. A reinforced armoured battalion would attack from the north, including Centurions under Natke Nir, against 'Oakland', a defensive position on Abu Agheila's northern flank. Once Oakland was taken, Nir would then manoeuvre around the rear of Abu Agheila, establishing blocking forces as he moved along the road to Jebel Libni, the location of the Egyptian reserves, the Centurions assaulting the base from the rear. With the battlefield isolated, Sharon's next move was to 'attack the entire depth of the Egyptian positions simultaneously', a move that would deliver the *taboulah* – an unbalancing shock. An infantry brigade led by Yekutiel 'Kuti' Adam would drive down the northern end of the trench lines, while at the same time divisional artillery concentrated its fire on the trenches immediately in front of Adam's attack. To the right of the infantry brigade, helicopters would deploy IDF paratrooper units, which would assault Egyptian long-range artillery positions. With the Egyptian defences distracted and under pressure, the 14th Armoured Brigade (Mordechai Zippori) would make a narrow frontal assault through the minefields, while simultaneously Nir's Centurions struck the Egyptian armour and trenches from behind. This entire complex operation would also be delivered at night, 'compounding the Egyptians' confusion as they struggled to piece together what was happening to them' (*Warrior*, Ariel Sharon, pp. 188–90).

This was no improvisational riff on Sharon's part. Although he personally had a somewhat maverick and aggressive reputation, his action in the Sinai was meticulously planned and timetabled. As well as Centurions, he had M50/M51 Super Shermans and AMX-13s.

Ugdah 'Sharon' actually crossed the frontier at 0815hrs on 5 June, advancing against moderate Egyptian fire and delaying actions, including the dug-in T-34/85s. The main action against Um Qataf and Abu Agheila, however, was launched at 2230hrs, opening after a punishing 20-minute Israeli artillery barrage, which provoked heavy Egyptian counter-fire. The attack smashed into blistering Egyptian resistance. The battlefield was soon alive with explosions, tracers and the tracking movements of the xenon searchlights fitted to many Israeli tanks, used to find and then engage their targets in the dark. Infantry battalions were equipped with special red, green or blue flashlights to act as visual identifiers between the tanks and assigned infantry units. While the infantry and paratroopers fought the battle at close range, Sharon's armour battered its way through the defences, eventually coming into contact with the Egyptian reserve armour in a pitched tank battle. Losses were heavy on both sides, with the IDF tanks also taking casualties from mines and infantry tank-killer teams armed with RPGs and recoilless rifles.

By the morning, however, the battle for Um Qataf and Abu Agheila was effectively over as the Egyptian defence unravelled and both infantry and armour began to pull back to the west. A similar situation was playing out across the Egyptian front. On the morning of 6 June, Field Marshal Amer issued a general order (without consulting Nasser or the chief of staff) for his units to pull back to the Giddi and Mitla passes, which were just 32km from the Sinai Canal itself. This was exactly the situation desired by the Israelis, who now had the opportunity to chase, catch and trap the retreating Egyptian formations. Still, the IDF could not afford to be complacent, as the Egyptians still had hundreds of tanks in the south of the country.

On 6 June, the Israeli advance picked up pace. Tal's units pushed from El Arish along the coast road towards Romani, and Yoffe's brigades attacked southwards against Jebel Libni, meeting elements of Sharon's division advancing out from Abu Agheila. At the same time, far to the south Mandler's independent 8th Armoured Brigade had pushed across the border to assault Egyptian forces at El Kuntilla. Although the Egyptians resisted the advancing IDF armour with tank ambushes, most of the Egyptian tanks were quickly knocked out in the resulting gun battles. The action in the south-eastern front served to keep large Egyptian armour assets confined away from the main Israeli thrusts further north.

At Jebel Libni, armour from Yoffe and Sharon's divisions fought a fierce gun battle with two Egyptian armoured brigades, again coming out on top from a long-range gun battle, before Yoffe pressed on east, heading for Bir Hassna and the Mitla Pass and destroying dozens of fleeing Egyptian vehicles in the process. A small number of Israeli tanks – just nine Centurions – made it to the Mitla Pass before the Egyptians reached it, and there the IDF crews fought an unrelenting engagement as the enemy armour tried to smash its way through to safety. Many of the Centurions had run out of fuel even as they arrived at the Pass, and had to be towed into position. By the morning of

the 8th, only four tanks were still standing, but they had held the pass and finally reinforcements reached them. Their resistance had generated a 5km traffic jam of Egyptian vehicles, which was bombed mercilessly by the IAF.

Meanwhile, on 7 June, Tal's division drove west on a central axis, seeking out the Egyptian 4th Armoured Division around Bir Gifgafa. A two-hour tank battle ensued, in which the IDF Centurions and Pattons gained the upper hand, before the 4th Armoured Division continued its retreat southwards. One interesting engagement took place in the early hours of 7 June, when a battalion of AMX-13 tanks locked horns with T-55 tanks near the Tassa Pass. The Israeli gunners put fire down on the T-55s at long range, but at this range and with a head-on orientation, their shells simply skipped off the thick armour. The T-55s returned fire, and demonstrated that the Egyptian crews were also capable of sound gunnery, destroying several AMX-13s and other vehicles. Nevertheless, the surviving tanks dispersed into the darkness and managed to work up on the T-55s' flanks, hitting the thinner side armour and destroying four tanks before the Egyptians once again resumed their retreat.

The Israeli advance was now unstoppable. By 2000hrs on 8 June, both the Giddi and the Mitla passes had been sealed, and by 0100hrs the next day the IDF had reached the Suez Canal. Despite having one of the largest tank armies in the Middle East, Egypt had been unable to prevent a truly catastrophic defeat.

JERUSALEM AND SAMARIA

Despite Jordan and Egypt being co-signatories to a defence pact, Israel began its invasion of the Sinai on 5 June with little expectation that Jordan would join the hostilities. Yet King Hussein, acting on misinformation from Nasser, was led to believe that the war was quickly tilting in Arab favour, and began shelling across the border into Israel from the West Bank. A new front in the war had opened. For Israel, although a multi-front war was tactically unwelcome, the Jordanian intervention did

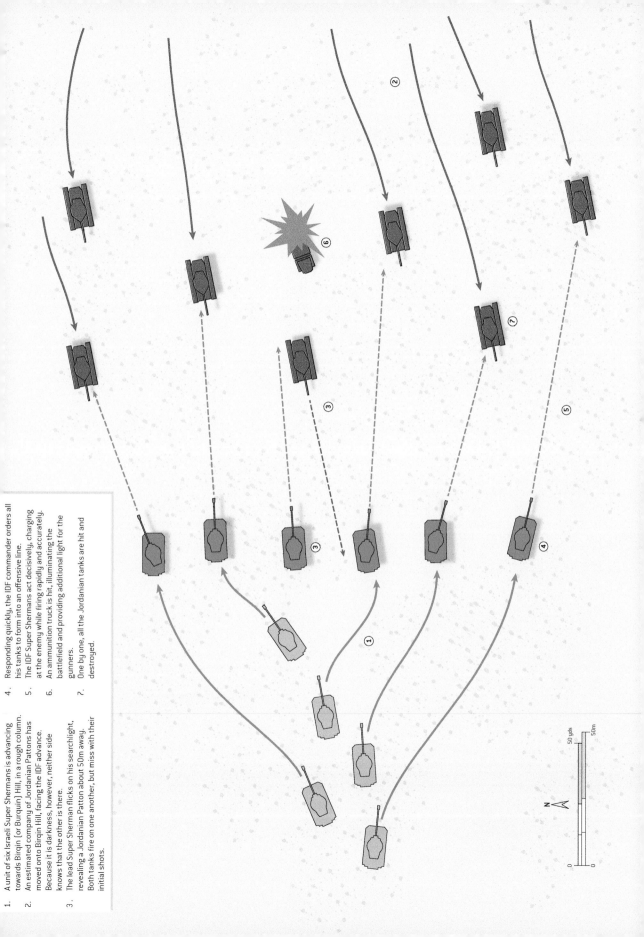

1. A unit of six Israeli Super Shermans is advancing towards Birqin (or Burquin) Hill, in a rough column.

2. An estimated company of Jordanian Pattons has moved onto Birqin Hill, facing the IDF advance. Because it is darkness, however, neither side knows that the other is there.

3. The lead Super Sherman flicks on his searchlight, revealing a Jordanian Patton about 50m away. Both tanks fire on one another, but miss with their initial shots.

4. Responding quickly, the IDF commander orders all his tanks to form into an offensive line.

5. The IDF Super Shermans act decisively, charging at the enemy while firing rapidly and accurately.

6. An ammunition truck is hit, illuminating the battlefield and providing additional light for the gunners.

7. One by one, all the Jordanian tanks are hit and destroyed.

provide a great strategic opportunity – to invade the West Bank and capture the holy city of Jerusalem, which had largely been in Jordanian hands since the 1948 war.

Supporting the 55th Airborne Brigade, the main IDF tank unit deployed for the Jerusalem operation was the 10th Mechanized Brigade, commanded by Colonel Uri Ben Ari, and consisting of a mixed M50 and Centurion battalion, an AMX-13 battalion and a half-track-mounted mechanized infantry battalion. The physical defences around and within Jerusalem were to be respected, and held by some of the best Jordanian troops. While the 55th Airborne would plunge into the heart of the city itself, the Israeli armour closed in on Jerusalem's defences from the north, where the Jordanian 60th Armoured Brigade was also located. On 6 June, the Israeli tanks successfully fought through the Jordanian networks of pillboxes, minefields and anti-tank guns, Ari sending his Centurions on a flanking mission as the rest of his unit pushed straight down the Jerusalem Corridor. By the time the Israeli tanks came up against the 60th Armoured Brigade, many of the Jordanian tanks had already been destroyed by IAF air strikes, and the shocked survivors were soon dispatched by Israeli tank fire. Furthermore, by the end of 7 June Jerusalem was fully in Israeli hands (after a hard urban battle) and the Jordanian Army was in retreat from the West Bank.

The other element of Israel's operations in the West Bank was the fight for Samaria in the north. Here, the tank vs tank battle would reach an entirely different pitch of intensity, one of the most violent and, for the Israelis, threatening of the war.

Samaria was not an amenable theatre for armour. It was rugged, hilly terrain, with narrow tracks passing through small villages in no way built with the passage of large armoured vehicles in mind. Orchards, groves and woodland further split up the terrain. Yet Samaria had to be taken, to alleviate the risk of a Jordanian incursion into Israel literally cutting the state in two.

Under the jurisdiction of GOC Northern Command, the armoured formation assigned to the Samaria action was *Ugdah* 'Peled', commanded by Brigadier-General Elad Peled and consisting of the 37th and 45th Armoured brigades. They faced four Jordanian brigades, including two independent armoured battalions acting in the support of the infantry and the respected 40th Armoured Brigade positioned with a large force of M47 and M48 tanks at Damiya Bridge on the Jordan River. The first mission for *Ugdah* 'Peled' was to cross the border and destroy batteries of 155mm artillery guns that were bombarding the IAF airfield at Ramat David. This objective was given to the 45th Armoured Brigade, which was mainly kitted out with M50/M51 Super Shermans.

The action began in the evening hours of darkness on 5 June. The going was hard from the outset, with heavy artillery fire directed against the advancing tanks and half-tracks and problems with traffic jams when moving through small villages. The IDF tanks came face to face within Jordanian armour around Birqin Hill in the strategically

The Harel Memorial in Har Adar, West Bank, remembers the battle of the 10th Harel Armoured Brigade in this sector of operations during the Six-Day War. The three vehicles are a Centurion/Sho't (bottom left – still fitted with a 20-pdr gun), an M3 half-track (centre) and an M47 Patton. (Josh Evnin/ Government Press Office (Israel)/ CC BY-SA 2.0)

important Dotan Valley, on the approaches to the city of Jenin. The 37th Armoured Brigade also had a brutal day and evening of fighting in and around the Dotan Valley as it advanced east of Jenin. It found itself locked in long-range duels with skilled Jordanian armour crews, whose tanks were emplaced on high ground with commanding views of the valley. At one point, the commander of the 37th Armoured Brigade, Colonel Uri Ram, even sent small units down into the valley to draw fire, the other IDF tank crews spotting the enemy tank muzzle flashes and engaging them accurately. During the evening, the IAF unleashed ordnance upon the Jordanian tank positions, and the 37th was eventually able to move forward and take Tubas and occupy the tactically important Kabatiya Junction, destroying six defending M47 Pattons in the process.

But now, for the Israelis, came the most dangerous moment of the Samarian campaign. The Jordanian 40th Armoured Brigade launched a skilfully conceived two-pronged counter-attack, the reinforced 4th Tank Battalion driving up from the south towards Kabatiya Junction, while the 2nd Tank Battalion drove in from the south-west via Nablus towards Arabeh. If the two prongs were coordinated properly, they would trap much of the Israel armoured and mechanized forces in a great pincer trap.

The IDF tankers soon found themselves fighting for their lives against the advancing arms of the 40th Armoured, the Jordanians' M48 tanks, also of more modern design than the IDF Shermans. The 45th Armoured Brigade was in particular peril, so its commander, Colonel Moshe Bril, pulled back from its offensive action against Jenin and took up a defensive position on high ground. Attacks on the 4th Tank Battalion by IAF sorties slowed the pace of the Jordanian attack somewhat, but then the Jordanians made a powerful attack, the 4th Tank Battalion making a frontal assault on the Israeli armour while the 2nd Tank Battalion swung in from Arabeh.

Rising to the level of threat, the IDF tank crews now demonstrated the excellence of their gunnery, hitting multiple Pattons on the approach and bringing the frontal attack to a halt. Eshel recounts the drama of what happened next:

> But the worst was yet to come for the Jordanians, as an Israeli armoured column worked itself uphill, using an uncharted goat track, and reached the main road by darkness, engaging the enemy armour from its rear. Skirting around an anti-tank roadblock, the Israeli Centurions and AMX-13 tanks surprised the Jordanians in a sharp tank battle, which lasted through the night. The Israelis knocked out 35 Jordanian Pattons. By morning, the proud Jordanian 40th Armoured Brigade ceased to exist, the shocked survivors, including the brigadier, making their way on foot to the Jordan bridges. (Eshel 1989, p. 84)

This victory, achieved at devastating cost to the Jordanian armoured forces, was one of the last gasps of a collapsing Jordanian defence. By the end of 7 June, the battle for the West Bank and Samaria was effectively over, Israel having acquired a large new slab of territory plus the great prize, the holy city of Jerusalem.

GOLAN HEIGHTS

The battle for the Golan Heights actually began just as the Sinai campaign was coming to its conclusion. Syria had outlined a plan for a major offensive into northern Israel,

An AMX-13/75 moves through Tiberias, on the western shore of the Sea of Galilee, on its way to the Syrian border prior to the launch of operations. This front view illustrates the narrow width of the French tank – just 2.5m – as opposed to, for example, the 3.39m of a Centurion. (Ram Lahover/Government Press Office (Israel)/CC BY-SA 4.0)

codenamed *Amaliat Natzer*, but from 5 to 9 June the Syrian forces largely contented themselves with cross-border artillery fire. They occupied, however, deeply embedded defensive positions along the mountainous 80km front, with only three main roads/tracks – themselves mined – winding up the Golan through precipitous and difficult terrain towards heavily defended positions sunk into the rock and soil, bristling with anti-tank guns. Anyone thinking about attempting an armoured/infantry assault to clear these positions would be labouring under multiple disadvantages from the start. Yet on 9 June, that is just what the IDF sought to do, looking to clear the threat on its northern border.

Regarding the armour available for this operation, IDF Northern Command had Major-General Mandler's 8th Armoured Brigade, which had now made a 350km road move from its operations in the Negev Desert; both of its battalions were understrength. The command also had the organic Sherman support in the 1st Golani Infantry Brigade (the main assault formation), plus a Sherman tank battalion from the 37th Armoured Brigade. On the other side, the Syrians possessed about 750 tanks in total, mostly a mix of T-34/85s and T-54s, and a handful of PzKpfw IVs. Many of these tanks were held to the rear

An Israeli M50 Super Sherman pushes through the gates of a Syrian Army camp on the outskirts of Kuneitra. Just below the turret, with their heads out of their hatches, we see the driver (viewer's right) and the assistant driver/bow machine gunner. (Moshe Milner/Government Press Office (Israel)/CC BY-SA 4.0)

as a reserve, although each of the six infantry brigades deployed on the heights included an armoured battalion, with 40 T-34/85s and T-54s, and the immediate armoured reserve in the form of the 14th and 44th Armoured battalions.

The Israeli plan, in basic outline, was for a multi-pronged assault onto the Golan. The main attack in the north would be conducted by *Ugdah* 'Laner', in which the 8th Armoured Brigade and the 1st Golani Infantry Brigade was formed into three battlegroups:

1. The 129th Tank Battalion with attached infantry and brigade headquarters, which was to assault Sir Adib and Qala;
2. The 12th Barak Infantry Battalion with attached armour, whose main objectives were Banias and the headwaters of the Banias River, taking the powerful Tel Fahr defences on the way;
3. The 51st Infantry Battalion with an attached company of M50 Shermans, whose primary initial objective was the Tel Azzaziat stronghold before driving east (Dunstan 2009, pp. 70–77).

By the end of the day, the IDF aimed to capture the village of Zaoura, about 16km from their starting points. The 45th Mechanized Brigade would reinforce the northern sector and the 37th Armoured Brigade would assault the centre of the front, opposite Rawiya, Nafakh and Alleiqa, while the southern part of the front was the responsibility of the 2nd and 3rd Infantry brigades and the 55th Paratrooper Brigade.

The IDF attack began early on the morning of 9 June. From the outset, it was agonizing going for the Israeli armour. Not only were they having to negotiate tracks scarcely accessible to a small car, with precipitous drops to the side (many vehicles were disabled or destroyed simply through accidents) and almost zero visibility from the dust and smoke, but the fire coming from above was unrelenting and accurate. Most of the shells came from anti-tank guns and field artillery, but dug-in Syrian tanks also added direct-fire input. Under the Syrian sights, the tanks also had to make frequent, vulnerable stops while engineers cleared stretches of terrain of mines.

Casualties rapidly mounted, and many tanks were lost on the way up the slopes, but nevertheless the survivors closed on the enemy redoubts. At Tel Fahr, for example, almost all of the Shermans supporting the Golani infantry were lost on the way up, although one that did make it to the perimeter gave good service by destroying a PzKpfw IV that had been emplaced near the entrance. At Qala, the 129th Tank Battalion was undergoing a horrendous advance. To give a sense of what this experience was like for the Israeli crews, here Lieutenant Nataniel Horowitz of the battalion's A Company describes just one of many terrifying moments in the battle:

> We came up to an outer layer of 'Dragon's teeth' [a concrete anti-tank obstacle] that blocked the road when I saw [Captain] Ilan's tank skidding off the road and falling into the valley below. The entire battle area was now engulfed in fire and smoke, with shells and bullets flying everywhere. Here and there I could see another of my dwindling number of tanks being hit, the surviving crewmembers scrambling out to try and find cover. Over the radio I ordered all fit tanks to assemble for a final charge on the fortress. To my great relief I also saw Ilan, who had miraculously survived, lead his tank in the charge, only to be hit yet again, his tank bursting into flames. But he had nine lives and he jumped down, put out the flames licking around his coverall, then jumped back into his burning tank! I watched as he then traversed the gun, fired a shot which destroyed the enemy anti-tank gun which had hit him. Then, badly wounded, he sought cover in the boulders, ducking from enemy bullets. And he survived! (Quoted in Dunstan 2009b, p. 75)

Mandler, seeing the grinding progress of his frontal attack, left the 129th to continue its fight while taking the rest of his brigade on a long loop around through Zaoura to

A well-known image of Super Shermans advancing up a narrow track on the Golan Heights. The status of the AMX-13 on the right is unclear; even the lighter types of armour could struggle to climb such steep, crumbling surfaces. (Assaf Kutin/Government Press Office (Israel)/CC BY-SA 4.0)

The commander of an M51 Super Sherman scans for targets as his unit advances into Syrian territory. The Hebrew letter and number next to the company chevron indicate the individual tank number and the platoon. (Vittoriano Rastelli/Corbis via Getty Images)

attack Qala from the rear. By nightfall, the brigade had met up at Qala and finally cleared the position during the night.

By this time, however, the Syrian forces were already in collapse and retreat. Although many IDF tanks had been destroyed or disabled in the action, relatively few had been the result of straight-out tank vs tank mobile combat. Most of the Syrian armour they encountered was dug in and largely static, acting more like turreted anti-tank guns. Furthermore, the major Syrian armoured reserves further to the east had been savaged by sorties from the IAF on the first day of the Golan operation, many units rendered ineffective before they even had the chance to move forward into action. At 1800hrs on 10 June, a ceasefire was called, and Israel had added the Golan Heights to its territorial conquests.

This image graphically illustrates the perils of vehicular operations on the Golan Heights – an Israeli armoured vehicle lies upside down after tumbling down a steep hillside. The Israelis lost a significant number of vehicles to accidents in the Golan theatre, rather than enemy fire. (PIERRE GUILLAUD/AFP via Getty Images)

ANALYSIS

The armoured battles of the Six-Day War should not be painted as too one-sided. Yet the statistics of defeat speak of an undeniable Israeli superiority. In the Sinai campaign, Egypt lost an estimated 10,000 troops and some 700 tanks (including 100 captured intact by the Israelis), almost completely gutting their armoured force. By contrast, Israel in the Sinai took 1,738 casualties and lost 122 tanks. Even allowing for some disparity in numbers between the two sides, these figures are still massively stacked in Israel's favour. The fighting against Jordan and against Syria on the Golan Heights was actually more costly for the IDF, reflecting both the professionalism of the Jordanian Army and the stubborn resilience of the Syrian positions on the Golan Heights. Against Jordan, the IDF Armour Corps lost 112 tanks, and a heavy 160 against the Syrian positions. On the other sides, Jordan lost 256 tanks and Syria about 100.

We must tread warily when deriving conclusions from overall tank losses, as they can mask some realities. For example, tank casualties included losses to all causes, and these include factors well beyond tank vs tank engagements. On the Egyptian side, for example, many tanks ran out of fuel or broke down because of mechanical problems, particularly during the long, hot and grinding retreat across the Sinai. Numerous Arab tanks were also killed by ground-attack sorties from the IAF, which often worked in close cooperation with the spearheads of the Israeli advances. For the Israelis, a high percentage of its armoured combat losses were taken from artillery fire and mines, through which the IDF had to push its advances at almost every stage. In the Golan Heights, many armoured vehicles were also lost after breaking down or crashing down hillsides during the approaches to their elevated objectives. Thus, what we cannot do is take the bare figures of armoured losses and extrapolate these to claim the relative superiority of Israel's armour against that of the Arabs, on a vehicle vs vehicle basis. What we can do, however, is make a more informed assessment based on tactical outcomes and the battlefield accounts of engagements.

We start in this direction by acknowledging an important fact: the Arab forces did fight, and fought hard. The Six-Day War was rapid, but it was not a walkover for the IDF, as the casualty figures above indicate. On all the three main fronts – Sinai, West Bank and Golan Heights – Arab soldiers, including armoured forces, fought with tenacity and courage. Yet in the main, in tank vs tank clashes the IDF armour almost always came out on top. Why? We can point to four main reasons.

An Israeli M50 Super Sherman moves through a crossroads on the West Bank, with famous locations to the east indicated by the signposts. The Sherman hulls used to create the Super Sherman tanks could vary, including the M4, M4A2 and M4A3. (Bettmann via Getty Images)

GUNNERY

The IDF generally demonstrated superior gunnery skills, particularly in long-range first-round kills and in reloading speeds, both talents reinforced by lengthy and frequent periods of pre-war gunnery training, which was neglected on the Egyptian side in particular. Nor does technology alone explain this advantage. Eshel points out that 90mm Patton crews in the Sinai engaged IS-3 tanks – which had far more powerful 122mm guns – yet in some engagements still managed to knock out all the heavy Egyptian tanks with no losses. As we saw in the combat account above, AMX-13 tanks even beat T-54 and T-55 tanks in open battle, a fight that on a technological level should have been totally stacked in favour of the Egyptians.

SPEED AND MANOEUVRE

With the exception of the Jordanian front, where Arab armour forces performed aggressive offensive actions, the Arab tanks in the Six-Day War were primarily used in relatively static roles, which limited their capability for manoeuvre. Many tanks were subordinated to infantry formations, whose commanders saw armour more in terms of defensive firepower support rather than an offensive arm in its own right. Often, tanks were dug in or assigned fixed positions, a placement that severely limited their capability of responding to the fast Israeli pace and which opened up numerous opportunities for the IDF to make flanking or pincer movements. Notably, the IDF armour also placed a premium on rapid, deep penetrations, as we saw in the advance to El Arish and the closures of the passes on the approach to the Suez Canal. As a general problem, the

A knocked-out AMX-13 is inspected by Israeli troops on the Syrian front. Artillery was the real killer of IDF armour on the Golan Heights. In total, the Syrians had more than 260 artillery pieces emplaced to face the Israeli offensive in June 1967. (Express/Getty Images)

Arab armour was capable in the defence, but once Israeli formations had penetrated their positions and moved to the rear, the response was chaotic and uncoordinated. The IDF penetrations on the first day alone meant that the sizeable armoured reserve held back by the Egyptians – some 400 tanks – was unable to enter the fray in a timely fashion, and when the main counter-attack came from the 4th Armoured Division it was already too late, and overwhelmed by the multi-prong Israeli advance. The most capable handling of Arab armour during the Six-Day War came with the Jordanian 40th Armoured Brigade's pincer attack in Samaria, but even this was eventually stopped by IDF fire and manoeuvre.

LEADERSHIP

In the Sinai, the Arab armour paid the price of poor senior leadership. At the moment the Six-Day War began, the Egyptian forces had little in the way of a clear war plan, at least one that could be actively implemented. Moreover, the defensive mindset noted above meant that the front-line armoured commanders had no effective tactical framework of response once the IDF tanks and infantry had cut through the forward positions. Combine that with a general lack of coordination between formations, and the outcome was almost predictable.

On the IDF side, by contrast, the standards of armour leadership were superb at every level. The *ugdah* commanders – Tal, Yoffe and Sharon – were outstanding men of war, who wielded their armour with all the textbook ingredients of victory: surprise, speed and tempo (some crews operated for 60 hours straight without sleep), firepower, manoeuvre. But the high levels of tactical training that ran down through all the ranks of the IDF meant that Israeli armoured units remained highly resilient in the face of officer losses. The distribution of the mission objectives, down to the lowest levels and the tacit permission to adapt plans and objectives on the hoof, meant that subordinates would simply pick up the baton and keep the operation moving.

Within the Egyptian forces, such initiative was generally lacking, as was a sense of battlefield awareness. The latter was demonstrated visibly by the fact that Arab tank crews in general largely fought with their tanks 'buttoned up', the commander and crew down inside the tank with the hatches closed. The IDF commanders, by contrast, tended to ride out the battle stood up in open hatches. This was a very dangerous practice, as it exposed them to all the flying ordnance outside, and many commanders did indeed die in position. The major advantage, though, was that it gave the commander a superb all-round awareness of the battlefield, leading at times to better, more instinctive decisions in response to situational evolutions. It was another example of the Israeli way of war.

An Israeli soldier inspects the astonishingly contorted wreckage of an armoured vehicle on the road between Bethlehem and Jerusalem in June 1967. The Super Sherman to the right has rotated its turret to face out over the rear hull, a position that reduces the amount of clearance required for turning. (PIERRE GUILLAUD/AFP via Getty Images)

SUPPORT

Armour does not win on its own. It would be an act of conceptual tunnel vision to explain the victories of the IDF Armour Corps in the Six-Day War purely in terms of armoured competence. An undeniably crucial factor in the outcome was IAF close air support, which, following the IAF's effective destruction of the Arab air forces within the first few hours of the campaign, enjoyed near-total air superiority. Some statistics from a US quantitative study of the 1967 and 1973 Arab–Israeli wars illustrate the point. The following tables present both the estimated daily tank casualties on each front and also the number of CAS sorties flown each day (source: HERO 1976).

Sinai Front tank losses, estimated by day		
Day	Israel	Egypt
5 June	51	250
6 June	15	60
7 June	41	190
8 June	15	200

Sinai Front, estimated CAS air sorties		
Day	Israel	Egypt
5 June	78	61
6 June	152	20
7 June	152	0
8 June	245	0

Jordan Front tank losses, estimated by day		
Day	Israel	Jordan
5 June	38	90
6 June	46	100
7 June	28	66

Jordan Front, estimated CAS air sorties		
Day	Israel	Jordan
5 June	76	11
6 June	112	0
7 June	114	0

Golan Front tank losses, estimated by day		
Day	Israel	Syria
9 June	55	35
10 June	105	65

Golan Front, estimated CAS air sorties		
Day	Israel	Syria
9 June	238	0
10 June	231	0

The figures regarding the tank losses throw up some interesting data points. Note how on both the Sinai and Jordanian fronts, there is a clear inequality between the IDF tank losses and those of Egypt and Jordan, steeply in favour of Israel (although the IDF losses are still significant), while on the Golan Front it was the IDF armour that suffered the greater pain, a product of the fact that they were mostly fighting against pre-prepared and very heavily defended positions, across terrain that did not favour tank movement. Across all three fronts, however, the disparity in CAS between Israel and its opponents is stark. By 7 June, none of the Arab armies was able to fly CAS, whereas the IAF was delivering these missions in their hundreds. Thus a major chunk of all Arab armour losses was certainly due to air strikes, a factor that surely helped suppress IDF armour losses on the Sinai and Jordanian fronts. The fact that the air strikes over the Golan did not alleviate Israeli armour losses (or at least did not prevent them from being very heavy) is likely an indication that air power can have limited effects on hardened and hidden defences.

In every battle, the IDF armour was also accompanied by mechanized infantry. In fact, this was one of the few aspects of the Israeli operation that attracted more sceptical analysis after the war. The half-tracks in which the infantry deployed were highly vulnerable to enemy artillery and tank fire, and the standards of training amongst the infantry (although not the elite airborne troops) came under some criticism following the war. This being said, we must always recognize that the armour 'mailed fist' unleashed against the Arabs in 1967 was just part of a combined-arms victory.

Israeli M48 Pattons move en masse through the Gaza Strip. One of the distinctive features of the M48 and its variants was the commander's cupola, which allowed the commander to remotely operate the .50-cal. machine gun from a hatch-down position. (Shabtai Tal/GPO via Getty Images)

CONCLUSION

On 28 June 1967, the Israeli chief of staff and future prime minister Yitzhak Rabin, in an address given when receiving an honorary doctorate from The Hebrew University, explained the victory in the Six-Day War largely in terms of human factors, rather than material ones:

> Our airmen, who struck the enemies' planes so accurately that no one in the world understands how it was done ... our armoured troops who beat the enemy even when their equipment was inferior to his; our soldiers in all other branches ... who overcame our enemies everywhere, despite the latter's superior numbers and fortifications – all these revealed not only coolness and courage in the battle but ... an understanding that only their personal stand against the greatest dangers would achieve victory for their country and for their families, and that if victory was not theirs the alternative was annihilation.

Certainly, the motivation for Israel to win, and quickly, was extremely strong, and cannot be underestimated. When the price of defeat is unthinkable, people fight hard. He was also right to suggest that the outcome of the armoured battle did not depend purely upon technology but on the capabilities of the crews, although in balance a crew still needs an effective fighting tool to win an engagement.

In the aftermath of the war, military analysts poured over the conflict studiously, looking for the right lessons. To some, the war appeared to offer a comparative insight into Soviet vs Western tactics, although this perspective was flawed at the highest level. Neither the United States nor the Soviet Union wanted to be drawn into a major conflict in the Middle East, which would likely result if Egypt and its Arab allies successfully invaded, defeated and occupied Israel, or if Israel's American backing unduly affected the regional status quo. For this reason, US and Soviet military

An evocative image of M51 Super Shermans silhouetted against the desert sky during operations in the Sinai. Although most of the IDF Armoured Corps' commanders were seasoned veterans, for many of the young tank crews the Six-Day War was their first taste of combat. (Universal History Archive/Universal Images Group via Getty Images)

material support was primarily focused on providing tactically useful equipment, rather than strategically game-changing weaponry. For example, the Soviets resisted supplying Egypt with both strategic bombers and with surface-to-surface ballistic missiles, despite Nasser's requests for such systems. Tanks, on the other hand, were a tangible force expansion, but one that made most sense in defensive tactics or short to medium-range offensive tactics. In reality, both the United States and the Soviet Union wanted their Middle Eastern partners to be able to defend themselves convincingly, and little more.

After the war, in Egypt there was a genuine attempt at military reform, sacking a generation of nest-feathering leaders and attempting to develop more professional competence and flexible tactics. Crucially, the Egyptians under (from 1970) President Anwar Sadat recognized that to fight the Israelis effectively, it needed answers to IDF armour and IAF air superiority. To this end, the great Egyptian rearmament that took place in the late 1960s and early 1970s focused on integrating large volumes of anti-tank missiles and surface-to-air missile (SAM) technology into its army. It would be these weapons that would shock the IDF Armoured Corps in the Yom Kippur War of 1973, and which would dramatically challenge its confidence in the mailed fist of armour.

BIBLIOGRAPHY

Benninghof, Mike, 'Panzer Grenadier (Modern): 1967: Sword of Israel – The Six-Day War' (April–December 2019). Access to all articles via: http://www.avalanchepress.com/game1967.php

Bonds, Ray (ed.), *The Soviet War Machine: An Encyclopedia of Russian Military Equipment and Strategy*, London: Salamander (1977)

Dunstan, Simon, *The Six-Day War 1967: Sinai*, Oxford: Osprey Publishing (2009)

——, *The Six-Day War 1967: Jordan and Syria*, Oxford: Osprey Publishing (2009b)

——, *Centurion Universal Tank 1943–2003*, Oxford: Osprey Publishing (2003)

Eshel, David (ed.), *The Six-Day War, 5–10 June 67*. Born in Battle, No. 6. Hod Hasharon, Israel: Eshel-Dramit (1979)

——, *Chariots of the Desert: The Story of the Israeli Armoured Corps*, London: Brasseys (1989)

Foss, Christopher F., *Jane's World Armoured Fighting Vehicles*, London: Book Club Associates (1979)

Grossgold, Paul S., *The 1967 Arab–Israeli War: An Operational Study of the Sinai Campaign*, thesis, Naval War College, Newport, RI (1994)

Gudmundsson, Bruce I., *On Armor*, Westport CT: Praeger Publishers (2004)

Heikel, Mohamed, *The Road to Ramadan*, New York: Ballantine Books (1976)

Historical Evaluation and Research Organization (HERO), 'Comparative Analysis: Arab and Israeli Combat Performance, 1967 and 1973 Wars', HERO (June 1976)

Hogg, Ian V., *Israeli War Machine: The Men, the Machines, the Tactics*, London: Book Club Associates (1983)

Jackson, Robert, *Centurion: Armoured Hero of Post-War Tank Battles*, Barnsley: Pen & Sword (2017)

Marshall, S.L.A., *Swift Sword: The Historical Record of Israel's Victory, June 1967*, American Heritage Publishing Co (1967)

Perrett, Bryan, *Iron Fist: Classic Armoured Warfare Case Studies*, London: Brockhampton Press (1999)

Pivka, Otto von, *Armies of the Middle East*, London: Book Club Association (1979)

Pollack, Kenneth M., *Armies of Sand: The Past, Present, and Future of Arab Military Effectiveness*, Oxford: Oxford University Press (2019)

Tucker-Jones, Anthony, *Armoured Warfare in the Arab–Israeli Conflicts*, Barnsley: Pen & Sword (2013)

Weller, Jac, 'Israeli Armor: Lessons from the Six-Day War', *Military Review* (November 1971)

Westwood, John, *The History of War in the Middle East*, London: Chrysalis (2003)

Zaloga, Steven J., *Armour of the Middle Eastern Wars 1948–78*, Oxford: Osprey Publishing (1981)

——, *T-34/85 Medium Tank 1944–94*, Oxford: Osprey Publishing (1996)

——, *The M47 and M48 Patton Tanks*, Oxford: Osprey Publishing (1999)

——, *T-54 and T-55 Main Battle Tanks 1944–2004*, Oxford: Osprey Publishing (2004)

INDEX